IN THE NAME OF GOD

Entrepreneurship as done by

Ali Asghar Hajibaba

The Founder of
The Founder of the modern foundry industry in iran

Written by:
Dr. Reza Yadegari
Dr. Mahshid Sanaeefard
The Winners of the Prestigious
Jalal Al-e Ahmad Literary Award
and
Aryaan Yadegari
Lilyaan Yadegari
The Second Generation Authors of the
Great Iranian Entrepreneur Book Collection

- Introduction 3
- The Greenlight 5
- The life and world of Ali Asghar Hajibaba 7
- The analysis of The Founder of modern foundry 38
industry in iran

Introduction

The work of identifying the greatest Iranian entrepreneurs got underway back in 1997 with the help and assistance of my wife Dr. Mahshid Sanaeefard, the Manager of the Great Iranian Entrepreneurs Publication. An exceptionally long and arduous task, which has enabled us to gain substantial insight into the world of entrepreneurship and job creation, and thus make history for the future generation of Iranians by helping found and chart a whole new path towards true success in business and industry alike.

Next to winning numerous international awards on this incredible journey of countless ups and downs, we have cooperated and collaborated extensively with some of Iran's highly accredited and most reputable higher learning centers, like Sharif Industrial University, University of Science and Technology, Alzahra University and Shahid Beheshti University. Moreover, we have also successfully established and registered the International Qualification and Certification Auditors Company or IQCA in Canada, whose main role and responsibility is to publish the life history of the greatest Iranian entrepreneurs to make them known by name to the other people in the world. IQCA has also been highly active in setting up and establishing an award presentation scheme in Iran in order to identify and introduce the country's most creative individuals and organizations, and thereby aid and assist with promoting them on a global scale.

It is hoped that as a special and leading group, we are able to introduce the most powerful Iranian women and me to the rest of the world and at the same time, identify and retell the life stories of the best role models for Iran's next generation.

Dr. Reza Yadegari
www.UNESCO.ws
www.UNEBDO.ws

The Greenlight

The movement to transfer the experiences of the world's greatest entrepreneurs is one of the most important factors in helping the American and European companies and organizations' progress and improvement. These companies and organizations had concluded rather smartly that if a society wishes significant advancement and development, it must keep its eye on the experiences of the previous generation and not allow the young to incur costs on the system by experiencing and learning through trial and error. In line with the same notion, entrepreneurship has the potential to create notable transformation throughout a given society's various levels provided it is implemented using principles and plans that take advantage of the experiences of the proficient and skilled members. Allowing the young to take over across the world is certainly a commendable measure, which has also been taken in our beloved Iran as well, except that here the experiences of the previous generation of entrepreneurs and managers has never been made properly available for application by the new generation – something that has regrettably inflicted irrecoverable costs onto the country because of the continuous repetition of the same old mistakes. Our project to identify the greatest Iranian entrepreneurs, so that we may research their lives to understand the reasons and factors for their success started off back in 1997 simultaneously as the arrival of the novel science of entrepreneurship in Iran. Admittedly, the path has been a long one involving strenuous effort. In the years following the events of the Iranian Revolution, literary no entrepreneur in the country was willing to unveil and reveal herself or himself and the experiences she or he possessed.

In spite of this, we were quite determined to fulfil our goal of teaching and training the future generation by documenting and publishing the life stories and experiences of Iran's greatest entrepreneurs through a one-thousand-volume book aptly titled 'Entrepreneurship as done by …' What is presented in the book collection, is rare and valuable roadmap designed based on the experiences and performances of Iran's greatest economic minds, which undoubtedly can be a wonderful asset in guiding and directing anyone who intends to get involved in any type of commercial, production and service provision activity. We hope that our collection book can help open up doors and pave the way for Iran's new generation of young entrepreneurs, and also remain a lasting piece of literary work to remember us by.

Dr. Reza Yadegari
Dr. Mahshid Sanaeefard
Tehran, Iran 2021

The life and world of
Ali Asghar Hajibaba

In the winter of 1901, when the ground was covered with a soft, white blanket of snow, Ali Asghar Hajibaba, a dignified man, and his wife, Maryam Bisadi, arrived in Bozorgmehri Street (15 Khordad) from the village of Emameh in the Shemiranat region of Tehran. They settled into a beautiful home. The large, welcoming yard of the house featured a blue pond, and a single persimmon tree, with snow resting on its bare branches, added to the beauty of the scene.

The reputation of the Hajibaba family's nobility and integrity quickly spread among their neighbors and friends. These qualities were also reflected in their actions and behavior, and they were spoken of highly in all social gatherings. Ali Asghar Hajibaba became a beloved figure in the community, known for his admirable traits and kindness in everyday life.

In the home of the Hajibaba family, it seemed that a spirit of generosity and kindness touched everyone's heart. This affection was so genuine and deep that no one could ignore it. Anyone who met them felt like they were part of a larger, loving family. Mr. Hajibaba not only helped those in need financially but also, in difficult times, was always there to offer patience, compassion, and words of encouragement. In fact, his wife and family became symbols of generosity and nobility in their neighborhood, creating an atmosphere of friendship and kindness with their virtuous behavior. Their commitment to helping others and their sensitivity to the problems of the community earned them great respect from neighbors and friends, who admired their sense of responsibility.

Mr. Hajibaba, with his deep understanding of the emotional and spiritual needs of the people in the neighborhood, took actions that were more effective than any financial assistance. His support often involved offering guidance and counseling to young people and providing emotional support to struggling families. He was always present at various gatherings, and with his warm words and encouragement, he fostered a spirit of cooperation and solidarity among the neighbors.

This admirable behavior, which was inherently embedded in the Hajibaba family's nature, played a significant role in strengthening social relationships and creating strong bonds within their community. Indeed, just as these human qualities had made them a model for others, their words and actions can still serve as a valuable example for future generations.

The Birth and Childhood of Ali Asghar Hajibaba

A few years later, on October 1, 1931, in that lovely home, a little boy was born. With a heart full of love, the mother held her newborn in her arms and gazed at her other little darling, who was leaning on her hand and gently caressing the head of his newborn brother. Looking at her older son with a gaze full of affection, she said, "Do you see how beautiful he is?"

The boy, with childlike excitement, nodded and asked his mother, "What will you name him?"

With a sweet smile, the mother replied, "Your name is Ali Akbar, meaning Ali the older. So, we will name your brother Ali Asghar, meaning Ali the younger."

The eyes of the beautiful child sparkled with childlike excitement, and from the depth of his being, he asked, "Who can play with me?"

With a loving response, the mother said, "Whenever he can say your name as beautifully as you do."

Time, like a swift horse, passed the minutes and hours, and Ali Asghar grew alongside his brother. Now, not only could he play with Ali Akbar, but he also attended the "Entesariyeh" elementary school in their neighborhood, eagerly learning reading and writing with an insatiable passion. Now, in addition to his older brother and sister, there were a younger brother and sister in the family. Their father always advised them, especially Ali Akbar and Ali Asghar, to never leave each other and always be there for one another.

He would say, "Each child can break a single branch, but even the strongest men cannot break several branches."

Ali Asghar always listened to his father's advice and was never upset by it. He deeply loved his father, viewing him as a symbol of calm and unwavering strength. His father always had a prayer bead in his hand, softly reciting prayers. He owned a quilting shop in a street lower than their neighborhood. At night, after returning home from a long, busy day, he would hold a mourning ceremony. These gatherings became warm and intimate, where neighbors and locals would gather in solidarity. Ali Asghar, with curiosity, would stand in a corner of the room, watching the ceremony. He saw his father, head bowed, silently shedding tears down his cheeks. He knew that, amidst his tears, his father was remembering his lost friends and loved ones, spending moments with his broken heart. In those moments, Ali Asghar, too, would immerse himself in deep emotions. Life in that house was not only full of love and affection, but also brought hearts closer together by recalling humanistic values. In the heart of those calm and sorrowful nights, Ali Asghar would rush to his mother to share the sorrow that stirred within him. At night, after the mourning ceremony, the image of his father's relentless tears would not leave his mind.

He quietly asked, "Mother! How many times a month does father hold the ceremony, and the mourning speeches repeat? Yet, each time, he cries as if it's the first time he's hearing it. How can he not get tired?"

The mother, while washing the tea cups left over from the ceremony, gave her son a loving glance and, with a gentle smile, replied, "Because he believes in this work. In every tear, he displays his love and faith."

The next morning, when the sun's rays shone through the gap in the window into Ali Asghar's room, as he was waking up, he saw his father sitting by the pond, performing ablution under the bent persimmon tree. The sound of his father's reciting prayers scattered like a soft melody in the air, and when he stood to pray, Ali Asghar suddenly felt as though he was seeing him with a new perspective. He realized that a person can dispel fatigue by repeating daily the things they believe in.

The Teenage Years of Ali Asghar Hajibaba

In 1945, Ali Asghar reached the age of fourteen. He finished school and decided to go to his father's quilting shop to start working. Eagerly, he went to his brother and shared this idea. His brother agreed and, the next morning, they both went to their father's shop. With joy, their father shared his experiences and lovingly taught them the trade.

Working at the shop wasn't hard for Ali Asghar. With his brother's help, they sewed the quilts and took them to the market. Soon, his skill became so great that the people in the market recognized him well. One day, on their way back from work, when they reached the alley near their home, Ali Akbar stopped him and, in an irritated tone, said: "Wait, I need to talk to you. Why are you in such a rush?"

Ali Asghar, worried, said, "Hurry up, please! I'm so tired."

His brother continued, "Did you deliver Mr. Nasrat's orders to his shop today?"

Ali Asghar replied, "Yes! Father told me to do it."

His brother asked, "Then why didn't you take the money?"
Ali Asghar, trying to justify himself, said, "Mr. Nasrat isn't doing well financially; he said he'd write down the debt he owes us and pay it next month."
His brother, angrily, said, "You shouldn't have made that decision on your own. He already owes us, you should've told me..."
Ali Asghar gently responded, "I talked to father, and he allowed it. What does this have to do with you?"
Suddenly, his brother pulled him aside and slapped him hard on the cheek. Ali Asghar was taken by surprise; although they had argued before, neither had ever dared to hit the other. A heavy lump formed in his throat, but his pride wouldn't allow him to cry. Without saying a word, he walked quickly towards the house, angrily heading to his room. When his mother saw their angry faces, she immediately understood that something had happened. She went to Ali Akbar and asked, "What happened? Why is your brother so upset?"
While washing his hands and face by the pond, Ali Akbar answered, "Nothing. He's just stretching himself beyond his limits."
In a hurry, his mother went to Ali Asghar's room and was shocked to see him breaking open his small piggy bank, gathering the scattered coins from the floor, and carefully placing them in his bag. She approached him, anxious, and asked, "What are you doing? Can someone explain what's going on here?" Ali Asghar, trying to hide his tears, said, "Nothing, I just

want to leave."
His mother, worried, asked, "Where are you going? Who leaves their house? Where do you think you're going?"
Ali Asghar simply replied, "Anywhere! I just don't want to be here anymore!" and quickly ran out of the room. The moment he opened the door, he saw his father standing in the doorway. His mother, from behind him, said to his father, "At least you do something. The boys had a fight, and now Ali Asghar is angry and wants to leave."
His father looked at him intently and gently asked, "Where do you want to go?"
Ali Asghar, with a lump in his throat, replied, "Maybe I'll go to Mashhad, or maybe Isfahan. I just can't stay here anymore."
His father softly asked, "Did your brother say something?"
Ali Asghar lowered his head and, barely above a whisper, said, "Goodbye," and began to walk away.
His mother, crying, said to his father, "Why did you let him go? Why didn't you stop him?"
His father, with a prayer bead in hand, said softly, "He's not a child! He'll be back after a few days." And while still turning the prayer beads in his hand, he went inside the house. His mother ran to the door and watched as her son disappeared from sight, not stopping until he was completely out of view.
At the terminal, Ali Asghar checked each bus carefully. The evening was slowly growing darker. The busy terminal and the loud voices of drivers shouting made his thoughts scatter, making the decision even harder. He read the signs on the buses,

trying to imagine each city listed on the windows. The first bus was going from Tehran to Rasht, the second to Shiraz, and the third to... In the middle of his thoughts, a hand was placed on his shoulder. He turned around and looked. From the man's face, he could tell he must be one of the drivers.

The man briefly sized him up and asked, "Where are you going, kid?"

He didn't know what to say. For a second, he thought of saying "nowhere" and running back home. But then he looked back at the buses. The first bus he saw was going to Isfahan from Tehran.

He quickly looked at the driver and said, "Isfahan... I'm going to Isfahan."

The driver pointed to the bus and said, "Go to that bus, buy a ticket, and get on. Do you have money?"

Ali Asghar nodded and made his way towards the bus. The driver, sitting on the steps, was sipping his tea. Ali Asghar walked closer and said, "I'd like a ticket."

Without looking at him, the driver asked, "How many?"

"One," Ali Asghar replied.

The driver went inside the bus and came back with a single ticket, handing it to him. Ali Asghar dug into his pocket and pulled out the crumpled bills he had carefully saved from his small piggy bank. He handed them to the driver, then boarded the bus and sat down. A little while later, the bus began to move.

He had no idea where to go once they reached Isfahan. All he could remember was something a friend from Isfahan had told him at school – that if you set up a stand in front of a cinema, you could make good money. Maybe that's why he had chosen Isfahan. He leaned back in his seat, looking out the window at the dark, empty road. He felt tired and hungry, and without knowing why, his eyes suddenly filled with tears. With a heavy heart, he drifted off to sleep.

When he woke up, it was morning, and they were nearing Isfahan. A few minutes later, the bus stopped, and the driver called out that they had arrived. Ali Asghar looked at the unfamiliar streets. He was starving and noticed a café. His hunger won over his hesitation, and he walked in. The strong smell of cigarettes and hookah hit him. He sat down and looked around at the crowded, shabby place. People were staring at him like he didn't belong there.

The café owner, an old, bent man, came over and just stared at him without saying a word. Ali Asghar didn't know how to respond until the old man, with a thick Isfahani accent and a harsh tone, asked, "What do you want?"

Ali Asghar glanced at the grumpy face and asked, "Do you have an omelet?"

The noise around them made it hard for him to be heard, and it was clear the old man was hard of hearing. He repeated louder, "An omelet!"

"We don't have any!"

Ali Asghar took a deep breath, feeling even more regretful for being there.

"Give me whatever you have. I'm really hungry."

The old man walked away and came back with a tray of butter and honey. Without wasting any time, Ali Asghar devoured his breakfast. He then went up to the man, placed a bill in front of him, and quickly left. He pulled the remaining money out of his pocket and looked at it. There wasn't much left. Opening his bag, he glanced at the pictures of movie stars and the stationery he had brought from home. Then, he set off, asking the first person he saw for directions to the cinema.

The area around the cinema was crowded. He didn't care about the crowd rushing by and sat down in front of the cinema. He placed the empty carton he had brought in front of him, put the pictures and stationery in it, and waited for his first customer. He couldn't shake the feeling that he already missed home, even though he hadn't been gone long. He imagined his mother probably giving breakfast to his younger siblings and worrying about him. He also thought about what was happening at the quilting shop and what his father was doing. He wondered if Ali Akbar was busy sewing orders for Haji Morad. He told himself, "Maybe my brother was right. I should have asked Mr. Nasrat before deciding not to take the money. Father always said Ali Akbar, being older, should handle the shop's finances. Maybe I was wrong, and I should apologize."

He thought for a moment, then said to himself, "But he had no right to hit me. I hadn't done anything wrong. I told father I didn't take the money from Mr. Nasrat, and he was fine with it. Why did my brother think he had to be in charge?"

Lost in his thoughts, a child's voice broke through his mind.

He looked up and saw a woman with her six- or seven-year-old child standing next to his stand. The child was pointing at one of the pencils.

The woman glanced at him and said, "Give me five of these pencils!"

He handed the pencils to the child and received his first payment of the day. More customers came, and by midday, he had sold everything he had laid out. He looked at the money he had collected and remembered the words of his classmate from Isfahan. He stood up and walked through the streets. He visited places in Isfahan he had never seen before, including Si-o-sepol and the Zayandeh Rud river. He thought to himself how beautiful the city was.

He walked toward the Isfahan market and stopped in front of a quilting shop. He thought about going in and offering to work if they needed help. But then he remembered his parents and their worry. It had been a whole day since they had heard from him, and he knew they must have been so worried by now. He was sure Ali Akbar had also regretted what happened. He left the market and decided to go back home to Tehran. He went to the terminal, and as he was thinking about returning, his eyes fell on a bus to Mashhad. For a moment, the thought of going to Mashhad seemed tempting, and he walked toward the bus. He bought a ticket, and soon the bus to Mashhad was on its way.

Ali Asghar felt embarrassed and didn't know what to say. He walked into the house. His mother, father, and younger siblings were all gathered in the yard. His mother rushed toward him and hugged him tightly.

"Thank God you're safe. I've been staring at the door all this time, waiting for you to come back! Where did you go?" She glanced at his father and greeted him. His father smiled and replied, "Hello, my son!"

Then, they all went inside, and his mother set the dinner table. They sat down together and ate. As he was eating, Ali Asghar realized how much more he loved his family than ever before. After dinner, he returned to his father's shop and resumed his work sewing quilts. He argued less with his brother about work matters and made an effort to align with his brother's views on the finances.

The First Entrepreneurial Idea

Ali Asghar was getting better at the job every day. He had also become quite familiar with the ins and outs of the market. A few years had passed since he had left home, and now his younger brother, Qasem, had joined them. Ali Asghar was trying to teach him the trade. One day, after finishing their work, Ali Akbar and Qasem were called over. Ali Asghar stood in front of them and said, "I think we've gotten good enough at this work that we could open a store and send our products to other places. Running from one shop to another just isn't cutting it anymore." Ali Akbar looked at him and asked, "Where would we send them?"

"Maybe to other cities or shops outside this area."

Qasem said, "But opening a store needs a good location, it needs

a warehouse, and our shop is too small."
Ali Asghar said, "You see that shop behind ours? We can rent it. I've already asked, and the key money is two hundred tomans. The neighborhood below, you know, is where the Jewish families used to live, and they've all left for Palestine. We can rent one of their rooms as a storage space. What do you think?"
Ali Akbar smiled and said, "It looks like you've already made up your mind. Have you asked father about it?"
"When has father ever stopped us? If you're on board, he will be too. But we'll talk to him tonight and see what he thinks. I just can't do this without you."
Ali Akbar laughed and said, "Since I got married, I've been caught up with the house. I'll need to go back soon. You go ahead and ask father. Let me know what he says and what decisions you make."
It had been about a year since Ali Akbar had gotten married. He would come to work early and leave earlier than the rest of them. Sometimes Ali Asghar felt like his brother had changed a lot. He was now more responsible, more serious, and behaving like a grown man.
That evening, Ali Asghar and Qasem sat beside their father while he was reading the Quran. When he finished and placed the Quran on the shelf, he looked at his sons and asked, "What's going on? What do you need?"
Ali Asghar paused for a moment, then said, "Father, we've decided to expand our shop; we want to open a store and send our products to other places. Running from one shop to another just

isn't enough anymore."

"Well... how do you plan to do that?"

"Honestly, all three of us have saved enough to buy the shop behind ours. We're also planning to rent a room for a storage space. If you allow it, we think it'll be quite profitable."

His father paused for a moment, thinking, then looked at his son and said, "Are your brothers on board?"

"Qasem is on board, and Ali Akbar said he agrees with whatever you decide."

"Well... I think it's a good idea. You're no longer children for me to make decisions for. You know the market and the profits and losses better than I do. Go ahead and do it. And if you need money for buying or renting the property, count on my help."

Ali Asghar and Qasem kissed their father's hand and thanked him. The next morning, they informed Ali Akbar, and within a few days, they bought the shop and rented a room in the former Jewish neighborhood to store cotton.

Everything needed for quilting and mattress making was brought into the shop, and they stored the cotton in their warehouse. Instead of selling their quilts to nearby shops, they began selling them to different cities. They had many customers from all over Iran, and within a short time, they made good profits. Eventually, Ali Asghar hired several workers for the sewing, and he himself took on the responsibilities of finances and trade.

Two years passed, and Ali Asghar had been busy with the business, which was thriving. At that time, he never imagined that his career path might change drastically one day. He enjoyed the work and had long-term plans for it.

A Blessed Marriage

One evening, when he returned home from work, he noticed his mother and sisters glancing at him with smiles. Though he wasn't sure what was going on, he had a few guesses but decided to ignore it. His younger sister always said,
"Ali Asghar is so sharp and clever, nothing can be hidden from him."
At dinner, when his father had returned, everyone gathered around the table. His sisters were whispering and giggling to each other. Ali Asghar was about to bring up the business talk when his mother cut him off and said to his father, "Haj Agha, you know I'm not one for going around in circles. I'll get straight to the point. It's time for us to raise Ali Asghar. Mrs. Aliyeh, who you know, has introduced a relative of hers named Iran, a well-mannered and noble girl. If you agree and Ali Asghar is willing, I'd like to speak with her mother and set up a proposal."
Ali Asghar realized his guesses were correct. His sisters laughed, and his father agreed. He had no objections either. He had only seen Iran from afar a couple of times. A few days later, they went to the proposal meeting, but they didn't meet each other until the wedding day.
The wedding ceremony was held in the courtyard of the Hajibaba family house. The courtyard was decorated with lights, fruits floating in the pond, the persimmon tree looking fuller

than ever, and children joyfully running around the pond. The joy and excitement of the evening created the most beautiful picture for him.

Soon after, the bride and groom moved into a new home, which, if anything, was even more loved than the previous one. The new home, with its cozy atmosphere, brought a special kind of peace to Ali Asghar's life. Everything was going smoothly, and he continued his work with enthusiasm. His path was always full of challenges, but with strong determination and a heart full of hope, he overcame every obstacle. He also deeply cherished his married life, savoring every moment. The ease and tranquility of their life was thanks to the patience and kindness of his loving wife, who supported him in every matter and always stood by his side. This mutual understanding and teamwork made life even more beautiful for Ali Asghar.

The Uprising and the Burning of the Market

By 1951, everything had been going well. It was May when Dr. Mossadegh's premiership hit the headlines. This news made many nationalists, including Ali Asghar, happy.

Following Dr. Mossadegh's premiership and the nationalization of Iran's oil, massive demonstrations in support of him took place across the country. Ali Asghar, a supporter of the National Front and a respected figure in the market, also joined the support. He and many others who cared about the national cause wrote a petition to be submitted to the parliament. Ali Asghar, who had gathered signatures from many shopkeepers and market people, gradually became known in the market as a supporter of the National Front.

Those were tense days in Iran. People marched in the streets, holding pictures of Dr. Mossadegh, shouting slogans in his support, and for almost two years, the people continued to demonstrate in the streets to show the power of the National Front.

On the 28th of Mordad, 1953, a major coup took place, and all the shopkeepers went on strike, closing their shops. Ali Asghar, his father, and his brothers resisted the coup and closed their shops too. In the streets, the sounds of gunfire, screams, and cries were deafening. Many thugs were causing harm to people, and countless women, children, and men were wounded or killed. Ali Asghar had gone to his father's house that day. The fear and panic of the day had spread to every home. Qasem had gone out to find out what was happening in the market. His mother had a strange feeling of unease, and Iran tried to comfort her. Just then, Qasem rushed back into the house, excited and panicked. He ran to his father and brothers and said in broken words,

"They... they've all... come into the market... fire... they set fire to several shops... people are saying they're going to burn all the shops that went on strike."

The news made Ali Asghar's heart skip a beat: burn the shops?! Just like that?! The thought of seeing his shop, the cotton, and fabrics going up in flames and losing everything they had worked so hard for was unthinkable. That night was spent in worry and turmoil until morning, when the situation calmed down a little.

Ali Asghar went out. The broken glass from the previous day's chaos was still on the ground, along with torn papers and bloodstains on the streets. The newspaper vendor was shouting the latest news, that Dr. Mossadegh had been overthrown. Ali Asghar made his way to the market, and when he saw the burn marks on the doors and walls of several shops, his legs went weak. He quickly rushed to his own shop and was relieved to see it was safe. He sighed in relief but couldn't help thinking about the owners of the burned shops.

He opened the door to his shop, sat behind his desk, but couldn't focus on work. He could hear the voices of the people in the market talking about the chaos of the day before. When Qasem arrived, Ali Asghar asked him to stay and look after the shop while he handled the customer orders. When asked, "Where are you going?" he gave no answer.

Starting the Ironmongery Business

Ali Asghar walked through the market without really knowing where he was going. Lost in his thoughts, he suddenly heard the loud sound of iron being cut. Looking up, he realized he had arrived at the ironmongers' market. Since he was already there, he decided to pay a visit to his old acquaintance, Haji Qasem Hematani, the iron merchant.

He reached his shop. Haji Qasem had his head down, busy doing calculations with an abacus. Ali Asghar walked up to him, "Hello, Haji Agha."

Haji Qasem looked up and smiled upon seeing him.

"Ah, Mr. Hajibaba! What a surprise! How did you end up here?" He gestured for him to sit, and his shop assistant brought him tea.

For the next few hours, Ali Asghar spoke with Haji Qasem about the chaos of the previous day, the shop burnings, and their concern for their own shop. Haji Qasem nodded and said,

"Well, as long as your business is sewing quilts, you'll always have to worry about things like this. Why don't you join the iron business? These irons can't be set on fire!"

This suggestion made Ali Asghar think deeply. He recalled his father's words: "If you want to make it big, buy iron and cotton."

But he hesitated to discuss this with his father, wondering if after all these years of making quilts, his father would switch to selling iron.

That evening, when he returned home, he discussed the matter with his wife. Iran was supportive of the change, but she didn't know much about the iron business. She suggested he talk to his family about it.

On Friday, everyone gathered at his father's house. A few days later, Qasem's wedding was approaching, and his family was busy preparing for the ceremony. After lunch, Ali Asghar asked his father and brothers to sit down so he could share something with them. When he explained the idea, his father opposed it, saying that every business required experience, and none of them were familiar with the iron trade. His brothers also preferred to stick to their old business. Ali Akbar said, "After all these years of quilting, we can't just start from scratch with the iron business!"

Qasem added that now that he was starting his own family, his expenses had increased, and if the business didn't turn a profit, he wouldn't be able to handle the financial burden of his married life.

The reasons they gave made sense to Ali Asghar, so he didn't push the matter further. However, he didn't have a reason to dismiss the risk and believed in his ability to succeed in the iron trade. A few days later, Ali Asghar rented a shop and stepped away from his family's quilting business. His father and brothers were not upset about his decision to leave, and they wished him success in his new career, asking him to promise that if this work didn't suit him, he would return to them.

Ali Asghar first learned the ins and outs of the business from Haji Qasem Hematani and, after a while, began to work on his own. He cut the iron according to the orders he received, then loaded it and sent it to different areas. In a short period, he realized how much he enjoyed this work and found himself more passionate about it than quilting.

Two years passed quickly, and during this time, Ali Asghar advanced rapidly in his profession. Through tireless effort and hard work, he paved the way for his success, becoming stronger and more efficient every day. On one cold, snowy winter night, when the city had fallen into the silence of the night, something extraordinary and unforgettable happened in his life.

This special night was truly one of the brightest and best nights of his life because, on that night, his first child was born. A deep and overwhelming feeling filled his heart, so much so that when he lovingly held his tiny baby in his arms and looked into his innocent, pure face, a sense of joy and gratitude toward God filled him.

It felt as though God had bestowed upon him one of His sweetest and most precious gifts. Ali Asghar had decided long before this night what he would name his blessed child, and now, with this deep and soothing feeling, he chose the name "Mohsen" as a sign of his love and affection for his firstborn. This choice not only reminded him of his hopes and dreams, but it also symbolized a bright and loving future for his family.

The next day, the whole family gathered at their house, and the atmosphere was joyful. That same evening, Ali Akbar and Qasem came to see him, and when the conversation turned to business, they complained about the decline in customers for the quilting work. Ali Asghar said,

"Why don't you come work with me? The iron business is very profitable, and in a short time, my business has grown significantly. My only problem is that I'm working alone, and I really need skilled people like you."

Ali Akbar and Qasem eagerly accepted his offer with immense enthusiasm. Their eyes were bright with hope, and they asked him to talk to their father so they could join forces and have his approval. Ali Asghar immediately went to his father. His heart was full of excitement, and this time, with firm resolve and great enthusiasm, he asked his father to join him and his brothers in the ironmongery business, a venture they had dreamed of for years.

At first, his father paused and reflected. He thought about the current situation and the responsibilities this decision would bring. But eventually, a warm smile appeared on his face, and he gently responded, "This seems like a good decision. It's best if the profits from this partnership are shared fairly, and everyone values each other's hard work and effort."

Ali Asghar and his brothers were filled with joy at these words. They moved forward with this decision, full of happiness and hope for the future, and they began a new era of cooperation and collaboration together.

Hajibaba Brothers Ironmongery

A few days after Ali Asghar decided to hand over his shop to the landlord, significant changes took place in their lives and business. Ali Asghar and his family quickly, with strong determination, dedicated the two shops they had to the ironmongery business. In no time, the appearance of the shops changed dramatically; the cotton and previous goods gradually made way for a variety of iron products. A large and beautiful sign was placed above the entrance of the shops, reading: "Hajibaba Brothers Ironmongery."

Their activities progressed in such a way that, due to the greater appeal and profitability of the iron trade compared to quilt making, the Hajibaba family experienced greater growth and prosperity day by day. Cutting the iron, loading it, sending it to the market, and, of course, selling these products became the family's daily routine.

Although these activities came with their own challenges and difficulties, they ultimately led to significant development and success, transforming their lives.

Every time the family discussed expanding their business, Ali Asghar's mother would look at her grandchildren with a warm, loving gaze and proudly say,

"These children have brought good luck for us; they have brought prosperity with them."

These words not only reflected her love and affection for the family but also beautifully illustrated the hopes and dreams that each one of them carried within their hearts.

Importing Iron and Establishing the "One" Company

A year passed, and Ali Asghar began to consider importing iron. Like all his previous ventures, this also carried significant risks, but he and his brothers were skilled enough to manage it.

He first thought about establishing a company for iron imports. As with all his other ventures, he discussed the idea with his family. It took a couple of months to establish the company, and they named it "One."

Ali Asghar, recognizing his brother Ali Akbar's managerial spirit, entrusted him with the management of the newly established company. After some negotiations and with considerable credit obtained from European countries, iron imports began, and within a year or a year and a half, the imported iron was sold. The challenges and the expanding operations of the company and the shop led the Hajibaba family to hire additional workers, besides themselves.

One of these employees was Mohammad Bokharaei. Mohammad had a strange personality. He spoke little and worked a lot. It was rare for him to talk about himself or discuss anything other than work. During lunch, he would leave the shop and return quickly. Despite his young age, he was energetic and agile, and in addition to his skill and talent, he would offer interesting ideas.

One Thursday, Qasem entered the shop. That day, the shop was quieter than usual, and Ali Asghar was handling the shop's accounts. Qasem turned to him and said,

"I heard from the market guys that Mr. Taleghani will be giving a speech at the local mosque tonight. If you'd like, we can head to the mosque after work."

Ali Asghar agreed, and after work, they went to the mosque. Mr. Taleghani was explaining the Quran and then gave a speech in support of the National Front. Many people active in the National Front attended Mr. Taleghani's speeches. Back then, every Thursday night, Ali Asghar, his father, and brothers would go to the local sandwich shop after work, have dinner, and then head to the mosque, sometimes staying late into the night, listening to Mr. Taleghani's speeches.

One winter night in 1960, at the same mosque, Ali Asghar met Mr. Mottahari. Listening to his words, Ali Asghar and his father suggested to him that for security reasons, he and Mr. Taleghani should give their speeches at Ali Asghar's father's house. Mr. Mottahari and Mr. Taleghani agreed, and from then on, every Thursday, the Hajibaba home was filled with local people gathering to listen to them.

In winter, they would go upstairs to a room where around forty to fifty local people would gather, and during the summer, they would lay a carpet in the yard and hold the speeches there. Ali Asghar witnessed how people eagerly came and listened attentively to the speeches.

In those days, the Hajibaba house was open to the public, and the number of attendees grew day by day, from forty to about one hundred and fifty. The large yard space often couldn't accommodate so many people, and many stood in the street or outside the house, listening to the speeches.

Three more years passed, and Ali Asghar felt that his life was calm and growing. The love he had for his wife, children, work, and family made life beautiful and aligned with his goals, and every day he worked harder than before to build a better future. However, this peaceful routine didn't last long, and an event soon led his life and that of his close ones into a crisis for a while.

On one of the days in February 1965, Ali Asghar, as usual, went to the shop early in the morning. No one had arrived yet. The work was busier than usual that day. Ali Asghar knew Mohammad always arrived earlier than others and could help him get the day's tasks in order.

An hour passed, and as the others arrived, Ali Asghar turned to Qasem and said, "It's 11:30, but Mohammad still hasn't arrived!"

Qasem, busy loading the iron, said,

"He must have had something come up. He may be a little late, or maybe he's feeling unwell. Don't worry."

Ali Asghar nodded but replied, "He's never been late for even half an hour before."

Qasem laughed, "Well, I guess your sense of order is spoiling you!"

They continued with their work, but Ali Asghar remained worried about Mohammad not showing up. After another couple of hours, it became clear that Mohammad wasn't coming that day. Yet, Ali Asghar still felt a strange unease. As the shop closed for the day and the workers left, Qasem was preparing to leave as well, but Ali Asghar was still sitting behind his desk. Qasem turned to him and said,

"Thank God, all the work is done today and didn't spill over to tomorrow.

Why are you still sitting? Don't you want to close up?"

Ali Asghar glanced at the clock and said, "No, I'll stay a little longer. Maybe Mohammad will come."

Qasem laughed, "At this hour? It's already past closing time!"

"I feel like he's coming. He's worked here for a year and never been late or missed a day. Something must have happened."

Qasem shook his head, "I doubt it. But suit yourself. I'm leaving. Goodbye."

A few hours later, Ali Asghar looked at the clock. It was a quarter to 10. All the shops around had closed. Ali Asghar decided to leave too. As he stepped outside and began locking the door, he heard faint footsteps behind him. A shadow approached and quietly said, "Hello, Sir."

Ali Asghar looked and asked, "Mohammad... is that you?" Mohammad nodded and softly said, "Can we go inside?"

Ali Asghar opened the door, and they entered the shop. When he turned on the light and saw Mohammad's face, a moment of horror overtook him. His face was deeply wounded, with a gash from top to bottom, exposing the bone structure. He wore a hat, and his clothes were torn and covered in dirt. He was terrified, constantly looking around.

With concern, Ali Asghar asked, "What happened? What's going on?"

Mohammad, stuttering from fear, said, "M... Mr. Hajibaba... settle my account... I... I need to go."

Ali Asghar said, "Go? Why go? Tell me what happened."

"Please... don't ask anything, just settle my account, Sir... I... I'm in a hurry!"

Ali Asghar went to the cash register, settled Mohammad's account, and handed him the money. Mohammad pulled his hat down over his face and rushed toward the door. He then turned back and said, "Thank you, Sir... just don't tell anyone you saw me here... no one..." And in the next moment, he disappeared into the darkness.

Ali Asghar was shaken by Mohammad's appearance and words,

and his whole body trembled. He stayed a little longer in the shop, and once he felt a little calmer, he headed home. Iran was waiting for him in the yard, and when she saw him, she rushed over and said,

"Why are you so late? I've been worried sick."

Ali Asghar simply said, "It's nothing. Don't worry." And he went to his room. He couldn't sleep the whole night, constantly thinking about Mohammad.

Ali Asghar Hajibaba's Imprisonment

The next morning, Ali Asghar decided to go to the shop a little later. He had no motivation to work. During breakfast, Iran, as usual, had turned on the radio, and when they heard the first news broadcast, they were stunned.

The news announcer declared, "The Prime Minister, Hassan Ali Mansour, was assassinated yesterday by a man named Mohammad Bokharaei, an apprentice in an ironmongery shop. Fortunately, he was arrested last night..."

This news was so horrifying for Ali Asghar that for a moment, he felt like the world had turned dark. Mohammad, that quiet, noble young man, and now the assassin of Hassan Ali Mansour…!

The weight of these words was so heavy that he couldn't fit them together in his mind. The image of Mohammad's face from the night before, that wound on his face, the fear and terror in his eyes, the dusty clothes, and the words he had spoken, repeated in his mind. Iran said, "Mohammad? Your employee? What will happen now?"

Ali Asghar was lost in his thoughts when the doorbell rang, bringing him back to reality. Iran rushed to the door, and when she opened it, two police officers stood outside.
"Is this the home of Mr. Ali Asghar Hajibaba?"
Iran didn't know what to say. She stared at the officers. Mohsen, from behind the window, watched the officers, and the sound of Hossein crying from inside the room could be heard. When the officer repeated his question, this time with more authority, Iran nodded. Just then, Ali Asghar came to the door and said, "I'm Ali Asghar. Is there something wrong?"
The officer said, "You need to come with us to answer some questions." Iran, crying, said, "Why? Why should he go? What has he done?"
Ali Asghar went with them, and when the car door opened, he saw his father sitting inside. Seeing his father made him even more worried. They seated him in the car and drove toward the police station.
Iran, crying, hurried into the room. She called Mohsen and said, "Go to your father's room, and if you find any political books or documents, burn them in the oil stove."
They burned all his political books and writings. Afterward, Iran took Hossein in her arms and, with Mohsen, ran to Ali Asghar's father's house, where they found his mother sitting in the yard, crying.
Iran went inside, filled a glass with water, dropped a few sugar cubes into it, and handed it to Ali Asghar's mother, saying, "Madam... please drink this... don't worry... nothing will hap-

pen... they'll just ask a few questions. But for safety, we need to burn the books and documents they have here."

Iran, Mohsen, and Ali Asghar's mother went to the room and burned everything that could be used against them.

At the police station, Ali Asghar and his father were taken to the interrogation room, where they were asked about Mohammad. They didn't know much about him and said he was very quiet and always focused on his work. However, the officers didn't believe them and ordered their arrest.

For several days, Ali Asghar was kept in the dark and cold hallways of the detention center. Each day, he only heard the repeated questions of the interrogators and their cold, emotionless threats. Hours passed slowly, as though time had stopped in that cold, lifeless space. Ali Asghar, with a pale face and eyes that hadn't seen sleep, became immersed in his thoughts and memories. From the exciting days of busy streets and normal life, now only silent shadows remained.

Each question felt like a hammer hitting Ali Asghar, but he remained silent. Eventually, they decided to transfer him to solitary confinement. A dark room with nothing but cold, bare walls. In that space, the eerie sound of water droplets falling from the pipes echoed, and his only companion was the heavy, sorrowful silence. In his isolation, he stared at the dark walls of the small cell, and his thoughts wandered back to Mohammad. He remembered Mohammad, the young man with big dreams and a passionate soul. Ali Asghar repeatedly revisited their last encounter in his mind, his wounded body, his hopeful eyes, and the deep connection between them, evident in every word and glance. The feeling they shared in their farewell seemed to belong to another world. Now, however, revisiting these memories left a bitter taste. He couldn't free himself from thoughts of Mohammad's execution. Every time he thought about it, his heart would race, and his soul felt trapped like a bird in a cage. Each passing hour in that cell seemed to stretch into eternity. The seconds dragged on painfully, and Ali Asghar couldn't move. He sat hunched in a corner, sadly smiling as he thought of the sweet days of his life. He remembered walking among people without fear or worry, the starry skies of the night, the dreams, and the friendships... but now, in that cramped, dark room, he was left only with the memory of his days of freedom. The repetition of days and nights burned like a fire inside him. He hadn't been able to speak to anyone, not a single word had escaped his lips. Only heavy, sorrowful silence reigned in that space. Time had lost its meaning; perhaps the people outside had forgotten him. Only one cry echoed inside him: "How can I be saved?"

Ali Asghar had often decided to speak out clearly, but against those black, merciless walls, even words were chained. Inside him, hope and despair were locked in battle.

Conviction of Death

Two months had passed since the arrest of Ali Asghar and his father. During this time, the Hajibaba family had tried everything to secure their release, but it seemed that every attempt ended in failure, and the situation remained unchanged. Iran and Ali

Asghar's brothers went to the police station every day, pleading and begging, trying to convince the officers that neither he nor his father had any involvement in the assassination. However, no one paid attention to their pleas.

One day, as Iran and Mohsen were returning from Ali Asghar's father's house, they stopped by a newsstand. Their eyes fell on the front page of Information newspaper, where a photograph of Ali Asghar Hajibaba, along with five others, was printed with a bold headline:

"Five sentenced to death for the assassination of Hassan Ali Mansour!"

For a moment, it felt as though the world had stopped, and those few words paraded before Iran's eyes. The next morning, Iran, along with Ali Akbar and Qasem, hurried to the police station, asking to speak with the prosecutor handling the case of Hassan Ali Mansour's murder. Initially, they were denied, but after much persistence, they finally managed to see him.

After numerous discussions and follow-ups, and when the authorities found no evidence against Ali Asghar and his father, their innocence was finally proven. Information newspaper retracted its accusation of their involvement in the assassination, and a few days later, Ali Asghar and his father were released after two and a half months of solitary confinement.

These events had a lasting impact on Ali Asghar, and he became more immersed in his work than ever before. The day the news of Mohammad's execution spread; Ali Asghar was at the shop. For a brief moment, he felt as though he saw Mohammad standing right there, in front of the shop, sweating as he loaded iron onto a truck. That day, when Qasem returned home, he mentioned that Ali Asghar hadn't spoken a single word to anyone all day.

Establishment of the "Pars Metal" Foundry

A year had passed, and now Ali Asghar was determined to enter the casting and iron melting industry. After some follow-up, securing a loan, and with the support of his family, he established the first casting factory called "Pars Metal." However, setting up the factory required the cooperation and involvement of many people.

At that time, his father had retired, and his brothers were busy with the buying and selling of iron, as well as expanding their business and stores. Ali Asghar decided to invite a few people he knew, who were experts in the iron industry, to collaborate. After hearing his plans, they exchanged glances and said that, due to his young age, they weren't sure this idea would be profitable, and they declined to join him. This, however, didn't make Ali Asghar abandon his plans. He was determined to find partners for his venture. After some time, he succeeded in convincing a group of people to join him. Slowly, the large space of "Pars Metal" factory began to fill with electric melting furnaces, and Ali Asghar decided to begin production with water and sewage pipes and cast-iron fittings.

After evaluating the results of production, Ali Asghar realized he had taken a significant step in the iron melting industry in

Iran. Thanks to the high quality of the products, the number of customers increased day by day. The name of Ali Asghar Hajibaba and his factory, Pars Metal, became well-known. Some believed that these domestically produced products would soon replace European imports, and if this trend continued, in a few years, Ali Asghar Hajibaba would become the most recognized name in the foundry industry. However, they didn't know that Ali Asghar's plans didn't stop there, and he still had much larger ambitions in mind.

Establishment of the "Chauffagekar" Factory

It was early 1971, and although Ali Asghar had achieved many of his goals, he was still thinking about expanding his business and wanted to introduce new products to the market. With the experience and skills he gained from establishing Pars Metal, he decided to set up another factory, this time focusing on the production of radiators for heating systems. After several negotiations with a team of specialists, he founded another factory called "Chauffagekar."

Those days were difficult for Ali Asghar, and at times he had to work around the clock. His journey was full of ups and downs, but Ali Asghar had never learned to give up. He fought with all his might to reach his goals. His love for his family, his work, and the future he envisioned gave him an extra drive. Every time he thought of the growth of his business, his path in life, and his now five children, his indomitable spirit would rise higher than ever. He believed that the only reason for his achievements was love.

In 1979, after the revolution, Ali Asghar's work and life continued to prosper, though the loss of his father caused him great sorrow. That year, losing a father who had always been his supporter and protector brought deep grief to his heart.

A few months later, whispers of workers' revolts spread everywhere. Qasem, every time he met Ali Asghar, would talk about workers' protests in various factories. However, Ali Asghar wasn't overly concerned about this; after all, he had already faced much bigger dangers in the past.

One day, as usual, when Ali Asghar arrived at the Chauffagekar factory, he was confronted with slogans written on the doors and walls of the factory. He approached and looked at them. "Death to the capitalist" and "Death to Hajibaba" were written in bold letters. Ali Asghar wasn't upset by these words; instead, he felt pity and compassion for the workers. He wished he could share all the hardships he had endured and the long road he had traveled with each of them so they could stop their ignorant judgments and refrain from wishing death upon him so cruelly. Ali Asghar walked ahead, but soon realized that the workers had not only written slogans but had also stopped working and went on strike. The financial manager of the factory, who was trying to calm them down, saw Ali Asghar and said,

"Here they are. Now you can talk to them."

As soon as the workers saw Ali Asghar, a commotion erupted. They raised their clenched fists in the air and loudly chanted, "Death to the capitalist." Ali Asghar tried to calm them down, but it seemed the workers weren't listening. During the gathering, they made accusations against him that were hard to believe. A few workers threw large stones, shattering the factory's windows, and others targeted him. Yet, Ali Asghar felt no fear. Instead, he felt even stronger. He just wanted a chance to speak to the angry group who were harboring such misguided thoughts.

At that moment, a large man approached him, grabbed his hand, and led him into the factory, saying,

"Mr. Hajibaba... you're bleeding."

Ali Asghar looked at the man and recognized him. It was Mr. Shemirani, the factory driver. He reached up to his forehead and only then realized that blood was flowing from his head. Mr. Shemirani said,

"The stone they threw hit your head. We need to take you to the clinic to make sure your head isn't fractured." And so, through the back door of the factory, they headed to the car and drove to the clinic.

At the end of that chaotic day, Ali Asghar returned home. When Iran and his children saw him with his head bandaged, they were terrified and asked about his condition. A few hours later, Ali Akbar and Qasem came to visit. The news had spread that the workers had successfully expelled several of the factory's managers. Ali Akbar turned to his brother and said,

"This can't go on. You need to file a complaint against them. Don't back down. Today they broke your head, and tomorrow they'll bring even worse upon you."

Although Ali Asghar wanted to resolve the issue peacefully through dialogue, he had no choice but to file a complaint against the workers and decided to solve the problem legally. After a short period, the challenge was resolved, and Ali Asghar returned to the factory.

Establishment of the "Resitan" Factory, Manufacturer of Industrial Resins

In 1981, Ali Asghar Hajibaba decided to establish the supply chain for the raw materials of the casting industry in Iran. When he first discussed this with Ali Akbar, his brother initially opposed the idea, as he didn't believe the venture could succeed. However, with Ali Asghar's persistence and determination, Ali Akbar was eventually convinced.

To bring this grand vision to life, Ali Asghar purchased a large piece of land in Takestan city and, after importing reactors and other modern machinery from Germany, established the "Resitan" factory, the first producer of casting resins in Iran. Ali Akbar was appointed as the president and managing director of the factory. Once again, Ali Asghar Hajibaba turned his ideas into reality, and his name shone brightly in the industry. Furthermore, in the same year, he founded the Iranian Industrial Managers Association.

Establishment of the "Ferrosilicon Iran" Factory

Around 1982, Ali Asghar learned that the Revolutionary Council had passed a decree requiring the Ministry of Agriculture and Jihad of Construction to allocate land for the establishment of factories approved by relevant ministries.

Ali Asghar visited the Ministry of Agriculture and negotiated with its director, explaining that he needed about 50 hectares of land in Semnan province. The director glanced at him and said, "Mr. Hajibaba, the truth is, we can't give you this land."

Surprised, Ali Asghar replied, "But the decree from the Revolutionary Council clearly states that..."

The director interrupted him, smiling, and said, "Yes, it says that in the decree. But you first need to go to the Semnan Industrial Park and make a request there. If the conditions are right, we can allocate the land to the industrial park, and you can apply for a permit to establish the factory."

The following day, Ali Asghar, full of energy and determination, went to Semnan Industrial Park with his son, Mohsen, and his brother, Qasem. They arrived early in the morning, as the sun gently began to shine on the mountains of Semnan, filling the air with freshness and vitality. After persistent follow-ups and numerous visits, Ali Asghar successfully obtained the necessary permits and land for his factory.

Despite facing numerous obstacles, Ali Asghar pushed forward with his unwavering determination, and his hard work paid off. Thus, the "Ferrosilicon Iran" factory, the first ferrosilicon production unit in Iran, began operations in Semnan. The flames of hope and aspiration burned brightly in the hearts of Ali Asghar and his companions, marking the beginning of a new chapter in the country's industrial history.

Establishment of the "Iran Model Molding and Machine-making" Factory

In the 1990s, Ali Asghar Hajibaba, a man full of willpower and genius, made a decisive move: he decided to enter the mold and machine-making industry. This time, not only his brothers but also his children joined him in his efforts, and this collaboration between generations filled Ali Asghar's heart with a renewed passion for expanding his business. Observing the tireless efforts of the young members of his family, he gained a deeper understanding of his responsibilities, and this collective spirit contributed to further growth and success.

With his creative and forward-thinking mind, Ali Asghar chose a large plot of land along the Qom road to establish the factory. This land, once quiet and barren, soon transformed with the sound of workers and the vibrant rhythm of a new life being built. In this vast space, Ali Asghar built a legacy of effort and hope, and the construction of the factory began with enthusiasm.

Within a few months, the "Iran Model Molding and Machine-making" factory became a reputable and symbolic name in the industrial sector. The factory was not only a place of production but also a hub for nurturing ideas and developing talent. Inside the factory, the sound of hammers and the sweetness of hard work all pointed toward a bright future for the Hajibaba family and its workers.

In this environment, everyone shared a common goal, and Ali Asghar, as a compassionate and far-sighted leader, was always by their side. He welcomed new ideas and, with the collaboration of his family and workers, made significant strides in improving the quality of the products. The factory became a symbol of family unity and relentless effort to achieve success, while also telling the story of building a life based on determination and hard work, which, in turn, painted a picture of hope and a bright future.

At times, when surrounded by his family, now enriched by the presence of grandchildren, he would reminisce about the years gone by and the old bedding shop in the market. The factories that Ali Asghar Hajibaba had established through continuous effort had become his second family, and he saw them as his children; brought into the world, nurtured, and brought to fruition. For Ali Asghar, work and effort, which he had been accustomed to since childhood, were not just about making profits. What mattered most to him was serving his country's people and being unwavering in the pursuit of his dreams; dreams that, once realized, he considered to be nothing less than miracles.

Revitalization of the Iran Ferroalloy Industries Factory and Launch of Global Exports

In 2001, Ali Asghar Hajibaba, with his tireless spirit, added the establishment of the Industrial, Mining, and Engineering Exporters Association to his already impressive track record.

In 2002, amidst the daily grind and the challenges facing Iranian industries, he became aware of the troubled situation of a factory called "Iran Ferroalloy Industries." This factory, which had once enjoyed its heyday, was now nearing its end, and darkness loomed over its future.

Ali Asghar immediately recognized the danger and, despite the tough circumstances, resolved to revive this factory. After a thorough inspection of the facility, he made his final decision. This place was full of untapped potential and talent, and Ali Asghar put all his effort into breathing new life into the factory. With great courage, he faced the daily challenges, working tirelessly to keep the motivation and hope alive in the hearts of the workers and his team. Soon, his efforts began to bear fruit, and the factory resumed its operations with renewed strength and enthusiasm. This victory not only marked a significant turning point in his life but also revived a factory that had been on the brink of collapse. In the same year, he founded the Ferroalloy Industries Employers Association.

In 2003, as he reflected on his achievements, Ali Asghar, as always, looked to the distant future. He made a bold new decision: to begin exporting his products to other countries. However, the path was not easy. The economic sanctions that had cast a shadow over the country stood as a major obstacle to exports. But Ali Asghar never lost hope. Relying on his persistence and the support of his team, he gradually overcame the challenges and expanded his export horizons.

After several setbacks and continuous efforts, his products eventually reached distant markets such as Greece, Turkey, and Spain. Each successful export was a hopeful message, embodying the determination and resilience of Ali Asghar Hajibaba. He had truly planted a strong tree from the small seeds of his ideas, and through relentless hard work, alongside the support of his colleagues, he helped this tree flourish and bear fruit.

Loss of His Wife and Life Companion

In 2010, Ali Asghar Hajibaba, along with his children and grandchildren, took another step in expanding his business activities by expanding the Chauffagekar factory in Takestan. At the threshold of his 80s, with a heart full of enthusiasm, he still harbored grand and ambitious ideas. He clearly understood that for growth and success, it was essential that the younger generation, namely his children and grandchildren, gain the necessary experience and take on managerial responsibilities.

However, in the midst of these prosperous days, life suddenly revealed its harsh face. In 2013, Ali Asghar faced the loss of his wife, Iran, who had been his most precious asset. Her death was an irreparable blow to Ali Asghar's heart. For the first time, he tasted the bitter loneliness while continuing his work. Every Friday, he would visit Iran's grave, whispering to her about the passing of the days, sharing his sorrow with her.

And every time he returned home, he would murmur quietly:

Spring was here, with you, with love, and with hope. When spring left, so did you, and everything that was, faded away. This poem was a reminder of all the sweet and bitter moments of Ali Asghar's life and reflected his deep love for Iran. This great man knew that life continues, and he kept moving forward in the turbulent sea of life, honoring his wife's memory.

Ali Asghar Hajibaba's Achievements in His Eighties

Ali Asghar Hajibaba stepped into the dawn of his eighties with unwavering determination, despite facing various challenges and responsibilities. Serving as the Vice President of the Saman Industrial and Mining Chamber of Commerce, he looked beyond local borders with his sharp intellect, leaving a profound impact on the development of the country's industries through his work on the Advisory Council of the Minister of Industry. He was also an active representative in the Tehran and Iran Chambers of Commerce and was considered an influential and wise figure in the fields of trade and industry.

Ali Asghar, a man from the heart of Iran's industry, continued his international activities with steady and purposeful steps. Known for his broad vision and deep knowledge, he became recognized as one of the pioneers of Iran's casting industry. A few months later, he was elected to the presidency of the Ferroalloy Employers Association's Board of Directors. In this role, Ali Asghar took significant steps toward developing the ferroalloy industry by creating detailed plans and working effectively with other industrialists. He presented solutions that amazed everyone, based on his deep understanding of the industry's needs and challenges.

The hard work and innovation of Ali Asghar Hajibaba eventually paid off. The Iranian industrial community, in recognition of his invaluable efforts, awarded him the titles of "Father of Modern Ferroalloy and Casting Industry in Iran" and "A Distinguished Figure" in a grand ceremony. However, he never rested on his laurels and continued his work and efforts.

Love for the Homeland and the Path of Progress

Ali Asghar Hajibaba was one of those personalities whose vision of the future was filled with hope and great aspirations. His love for his country and belief in its potential always pushed him to find new solutions to help his nation. He ultimately realized that this goal could only be achieved through progress, innovation, and the establishment of modern industries. Ali Asghar never gave up. By establishing effective connections and collaborating with experts and specialists in other industries, he integrated creativity and innovation into his production lines and moved closer to his goal every day, making Iran's name heard globally in the industrial arena.

When asked about the secret to his success in production and industry, he humbly shared his thoughts. He considered faith in work as one of the main pillars of his success, saying, "We must believe in what we do. This belief is the driving force that propels us forward." He remembered that such faith and determination were lessons he learned from his father, and he always tried to preserve these values in his life.

In addition, Ali Asghar Hajibaba emphasized the importance of collaboration and teamwork. He knew that no one could conquer the highest peaks alone. By forming a team of eager and talented young individuals, he fostered an environment of creativity and innovative ideas. This collaboration allowed his business to grow rapidly, and his products reached international markets.

Ali Asghar Hajibaba, a man who shines at the heart of Iran's industry and economy, presented an incredible image of himself through his constant presence in factories and alongside large blast furnaces. Like an alchemist with a spirit full of courage, he walked through these vibrant places where metals, which once seemed worthless, were transformed into precious gems by his hands.

With a keen and investigative eye, Hajibaba paid attention to every detail of the production process and sought to understand all the elements involved. He thought not only about producing products but also knew in his heart that every piece coming out of those furnaces represented a life; a life of workers who toiled with their hearts and souls to achieve their dreams.

His behavior in the factories was as if a melody was being played. Every strike on iron and every spark flying from the furnaces symbolized the increased effort and love he had instilled in the industrial world.

Hajibaba wasn't just about production; he sought to create hearts that, with unwavering will, moved toward their goals and ideals. Through every word and action, he not only paved the way for progress but also inspired a generation of young people who were searching for a way forward in today's challenging world.

From a human perspective, what he did was more than just industry; it was a confrontation and revelation of life from a new angle. His deep understanding of the complexities and challenges of life led to the transformation of individuals and the shaping of a society in pursuit of progress. Ali Asghar Hajibaba was, in fact, a creator who with his own hands built not just metal, but love and hope.

The Passing of Ali Asghar Hajibaba

In the summer of 2020, at the threshold of his 90th year, this great man passed away. His name became immortal in the history of Iran's ferroalloy industry, and his loss had a profound impact not only on his family but on a great nation. Today, his children and grandchildren continue his legacy, striving to keep his memory alive in the hearts and minds of many.

The factories founded by Ali Asghar Hajibaba, with their past splendor and capabilities, continue their work without interruption. In one of these factories, in the management office where he once worked, a picture of him with a joyful expression and an inspiring smile is displayed. Beneath this picture, a small plaque reads:

"He who is brought to life by love never dies; our eternal existence is engraved in the world's book."

This poem clearly reflects his enduring approach to work and life.

Analysis of the Success Factors of Founder of the
Modern foundry industry in iran

A Healthy Work Culture

Many enlightened entrepreneurs in the East, and even the West, have succeeded in elevating the culture of work to a higher level. They have redefined work not as a difficult and exhausting task but as a pleasurable activity that contributes to both individual and societal development. When you hold such a sacred view of work, you will approach it with greater dedication. However, one point should not be overlooked: as Kim Woo-Chung once said, the assumption is that we must deeply love what we do; otherwise, the opposite will happen.

A Major Issue in Our Work Culture

Unfortunately, in present-day Iran, the work culture is not very appealing. Many younger people are constantly seeking jobs that require less effort, offer faster financial returns, and provide better opportunities. As the great Iranian philosopher, Allameh Mohammad-Taqi Jafari, once said, the greatest moral flaw in societies is when people seek results without effort or hard work. Therefore, it can be concluded that the culture of work in Iran has been largely neglected. As a result, both younger and even older generations are less motivated to engage in work, and as a result, tasks often fail to reach their desired outcomes. You must love what you do. When you love your work, it becomes something you value, and you will approach it with determination and seriousness. It is essential to reassess the work culture within yourself, and if there are issues, to address and fix them. A later and even more important point is that passion leads to extraordinary results. Many entrepreneurs have succeeded simply due to their passion, even without a clear vision or direction. Passion fuels enthusiasm, discipline, knowledge, and the necessary perspective. Therefore, you must not only value your work, but also truly be passionate about it.

How Can We Achieve a Healthy Work Culture?

But how can we attain the work culture we are discussing here? Everything starts from your mind. In other words, for these six reasons, you must love your work and consider it not just a means to make a living or achieve life's pleasures, but as a goal in itself. But what philosophies or ideas make it possible for us to see our work as a great goal, rather than just a tool? Perhaps these points can help you:

1. You must love your work because it has moral dignity.

If you do not work, you will not be independent. If you are not independent, you cannot have a healthy moral life. The condition for a healthy moral life is that you must be independent; otherwise, you will constantly be under the supervision, gaze, and control of others. As a result, you will lack courage. In the end, you will be a weak and humble person.

2. You must love your work because it has social dignity.

We live among the products and services others provide to us. So, why shouldn't we be one of the gears that drive society? If we don't work, we are essentially saying that others are working while we idle away. This is not a good situation at all; it is essentially the precursor to a parasitic life.

3. We must love our work because it has psychological dignity.

If you work and earn money by your own effort, you will have self-respect. If you do not work, or if you work poorly, your self-esteem will be shattered by the criticism and negative judgments of others. Do you think people who work well, progress well, and earn well have more self-esteem than those who do not?

4. We must love our work because it has familial dignity.

You've probably heard the story of fathers who do not engage in serious work. Essentially, men who are busier, earn more, and achieve more tend to be more important and loved in their families. Men who are home more often often lose their value in the eyes of their families. Of course, this does not mean neglecting time for the family.

5. We must love our work because it has a vision.

You may not love your current job. However, to reach the better jobs you desire, you must go through the jobs you do not like.

No one has ever reached the work, positions, or future they desire by sitting idle and waiting. Do you think you are exceptional in this regard?

6. We must love our work because it has entertainment value. Who says entertainment is bad? In fact, without it, people quickly wear out. Entertainment plays the role of oil for machines and devices; it must be present, or machines will rust. Work can actually be a great form of entertainment. Aren't there many people who, with their hobbies that have turned into jobs, create a lot of income and excitement for themselves?

Infinite Motivation for Work

When you think about these factors, you essentially realize the philosophy behind the work you are doing. Once you understand the philosophy behind your work, you will be able to adapt to how it is done. In fact, your motivation for doing that work will grow and grow. Motivation is essentially the collection of "whys"; why am I doing this work? Why am I doing it this way? Why am I serious about this or not? Why do I get tired of the work so quickly and not care about it? Why is this work so important to me that I am even willing to sacrifice my life for it? So, everything starts from your mind and thoughts. When you deem a task important, when you deem a task very important, you won't get tired of doing it, and if you face any issues, you won't just quit; instead, you will stay until the last ounce of energy you have. This awareness of the philosophy of work can also be a part of work culture. The same work culture that must be improved, and if improved, can lead to many successes. This work culture, if younger generations become aware of it, can help them accomplish more and show greater seriousness in their work.

Our elders in the field of business have often been renowned for their work culture. In the work culture they had, their words were, as they say, their bond. And you know better than anyone that when a person's words are backed by actions and there is a great commitment to making them a reality, it can be one of the secrets of building or rebuilding a brand.

Ali Asghar Hajibaba's Work Culture

The situation is similar for entrepreneurs like Ali Asghar Hajibaba. The fundamental question is, why do such individuals work so hard and endure the challenges of entrepreneurship in a country with many administrative problems and endless running around? The simplest thing for them would be to take their money and go to one of the neighboring countries and live comfortably, eventually commuting between Iran and there. In that case, they would have more respect and dignity there, they would enjoy life more, and their money and assets would be less at risk. Isn't that the case? But, as Kim Woo-Choong says, these individuals don't go through all this effort just for a few dollars, and the matter goes beyond that. They actually want to leave behind a precious legacy. As the saying goes, some enjoy food, and some enjoy feeding others. It's as if these people want to experience the true joy of life by sharing their success with others.

One of the managers and owners of private companies, who works hard and travels frequently, says, "My wife always complains about how much I work and why I need all this wealth." I keep telling her, "This is no longer just about me and my life; it's about the lives of 200 or 300 people, and I have to think about them." In reality, individuals like these no longer focus on their own interests. As Bill Gates says, when you become a billionaire, perhaps an extra billion dollars is as insignificant to you as a hamburger.

The truth is, as Brian Tracy says, money is a need based on an emptiness. People like money and praise it because they have this emptiness inside them. But this need remains as long as that emptiness exists. When you earn enough money, even more than what fills that need, there will be no more need for it. At that point, you need to find a different philosophy for your work. Although none of this means ignoring profit; profit is simply an outcome that will come and should exist. It's like the air needed for business and entrepreneurship; however, it's not the goal itself.

Chapter Two:
The Philosophy of Self-Sacrifice

A person, at some point, pursues personal goals; such as acquiring a nice house, securing a good job, building a substantial bank account, enjoying vacations, or chasing anything that directly pertains to themselves. But two things happen that change this person's course:

1. They achieve enough personal success and realize that these successes no longer satisfy them. In other words, they become saturated with their personal needs and goals.

2. As they age past middle age, they see that these things no longer fulfill them.

When these two things happen, they begin to look back at the path they have traveled. Now, they are searching for a larger purpose, a higher philosophy, and a reason greater than their personal needs and goals. What could this higher goal be? What is the motivation, the spiritual and psychological drive that will push them forward? Whatever it is, it's what can rebuild them after they've outgrown their personal achievements, and help them continue their journey with greater strength and purpose.

A Virtue Called Self-Sacrifice

Do you know one of the greatest philosophies and reasons for your actions could be a moral virtue called self-sacrifice? Believe me, we're not just repeating empty slogans or recycling things that have lost their meaning through overuse. Oyama, the greatest martial artist of recent centuries, believes that self-sacrifice is still one of the highest principles that has never aged, and it encompasses all virtues. He once stated: "Greed and selfishness make humans disregard others' rights and break the laws established for peace and harmony." He also said, "The only factor that gives meaning to actions and makes their effects eternal is self-sacrifice," and "One of the cornerstones of society's survival is when parents give up their personal comforts for the well-being of their children."

Kim Woo Chung, the founder of Daewoo, also said in his book The Streets Are Paved with Gold that he didn't work this much and sacrifice his life just to make a few bucks. Rather, he was pursuing a higher goal; prosperity and self-sufficiency for society. He considered the best years of his life the ones when, as a teenager, he went around selling newspapers, sometimes without being able to sell enough to buy food for his mother, siblings, and himself. But when he returned home, his family would already be asleep, and his mother would say, "We've had rice. This is your share." Kim, too, would lie, saying he had eaten soup outside and wasn't hungry. They both knew they were lying. These real lies made up the best chapter of the life of the founder of Daewoo.

In Search of a Higher Purpose

If you look at most successful people, you'll see that they think of a goal greater than themselves, at least one greater than their personal desires, goals, and wishes. This is excellent. The ability to transcend one's personal desires is indeed remarkable. But why do they do this? Answering this question gives meaning to their selflessness and transforms it into a powerful driving force. How does this happen? By thinking that a person has multiple roles and responsibilities, and fulfilling these duties leads to happiness and fulfillment.

These duties can be:

- Personal,
- Familial,
- Professional,
- Social,
- Global,
- Cultural,
- And more.

Therefore, we must inevitably feel that we are fulfilling our social and human roles, contributing to the greater good.

Making It Simpler to Understand:

1. For every success, you need to have a strong will and effort.
2. Willpower means sacrificing things that don't align with your desires and goals. It's about giving up short-term pleasures for long-term benefits.
3. Exercising willpower means self-sacrifice: you are giving up small but immediate pleasures for larger, future benefits that don't offer immediate gratification but promise fulfillment later.
4. For any success, you need to have the strength for self-sacrifice.
5. When this self-sacrifice is for the collective good, it becomes incredibly valuable, and all schools of thought and individuals honor it.
6. You should refine your intentions so that this self-sacrifice isn't only personal, familial, or limited to a small group but instead takes on a broader, societal, and human dimension.
7. In doing so, you'll find meaning in your self-sacrifice and will not stop.

8. The final outcome is that by not stopping, even your personal successes will multiply, and your actions will bring about a sense of happiness.

Everywhere you look in the world, self-sacrifice is happening:
• Ronaldo mentions how he gave up going to nightclubs, staying up late, and enjoying a comfortable life to reach his level of success.
• The Japanese used to sleep standing up in buses, so consumed by the effort to rebuild their country after the war.
• Michael Jordan, at the peak of his career, would be the first to arrive at the court and the last to leave.
• The Germans, as told by their Chancellor after World War II, worked with just a small sandwich and a cup of coffee until evening to help rebuild Germany.
• A diligent student sacrifices teenage pleasures to pass the entrance exam.
• And more.

From Self-Centered Intentions to Other-Centered Intentions
It is said that a person is made by their intentions. Now, if your intention for self-sacrifice becomes a social and public one, aimed at benefiting others, your self-sacrifice will take on a higher meaning, surpassing your selfishness. Osho, the Indian mystic, believes that life is not about ownership; it is about sharing. Those who live with the intention of ownership live in selfishness, but those who live with the intention of sharing experience the happiest moments and, through serving others and

humanity, they too become successful and joyful people. It's clear that with such an approach and mindset, you will never get tired. Gradually, your energy will increase, you will be happier, and even your personal successes will multiply, because, after all, the seller of perfume who sells fragrance to others will also be infused with its scent.

The Self-Sacrificing Entrepreneur

When we look at the life of Ali Asghar Hajibaba, much like any other great entrepreneur, we see the element of sacrifice and selflessness at its core. He was an avid supporter of Mossadegh, and during the period following the coup against him, Hajibaba was even threatened. During the assassination of Mansour, he was taken to the point of execution. After the revolution, the actions of workers influenced by some left-wing elements caused him significant problems. Any one of these challenges would have been enough to make any entrepreneur step away from starting a business or line of production. However, he was not someone who would stop. With immense sacrifice and selflessness, he started working in the foundry industry and made valuable contributions to the country. It was the result of these sacrifices that not only changed the wealth cycle within his own family but also benefitted the nation's industry and business sector.

The Wealth and Success Cycle in Families

In some of his books, Brian Tracy mentions that researchers

have studied the greatest civilizations in history and found some fascinating results. These civilizations began as very small groups and faced many challenges. Overcoming each challenge gave them more power, but more power meant bigger challenges. Overcoming larger challenges gave them even more power, and eventually, this process continued until the small group transformed into a vast empire. But as these empires reached prosperity, they focused on urbanization and ceased confronting threats, gradually weakening. Then it was the turn of another group to rise and overcome challenges.

Strangely, the lives of individuals follow a similar pattern. They begin in difficult circumstances, work hard, and overcome problems. Overcoming each problem leads to greater power but also more challenges. This cycle continues until these families reach wealth. However, once they have reached wealth, many families lose their goals and gradually lose everything, eventually returning to poverty, restarting the cycle. The key question here is, if such a cycle exists, why don't all families become wealthy? The answer lies here: in this cycle, there are always a few individuals within each family who rise up and change the cycle forever. This person sees the tough circumstances and chooses to take action. By overcoming problems and gaining power, they eventually bring the entire family to wealth, success, and great achievements. This is the point that can either lead to the downfall or propel the family forward. Surely you have seen many families where, due to the efforts and determination of one individual, the entire family's circumstances

change for the better, and their situation is forever transformed.
How to Avoid Falling?
But is it possible to prevent the downfall of families that have reached the wealth stage in this cycle? Yes. All you need to do is look at the life of Ali Asghar Hajibaba. He was able to break the cycle of poverty and average living conditions within his own family. However, he later decided to involve the younger generations in business and industry so they could also achieve wealth by working, not by merely having everything handed to them on a silver platter. In this way, wealth remains within a family and lineage, with everyone contributing to preserving and expanding it; even third and fourth generations, and so on. This is what Hajibaba did, and we can see the fruits of his work in the management of the third generation of his family.

Chapter 3:
The Culture of Entrepreneurship and Entrepreneurs

Footballers have their own culture, as do doctors, teachers, journalists, and many others. In fact, there are dos and don'ts in every field that help newcomers understand how to work and what values they should adhere to. The same applies to entrepreneurship; there are principles to follow. Although the ultimate goal of entrepreneurship is profit generation for the continuity of a business, the main motivation and driving force is not purely profit-driven, though profit is always considered. In reality, when you have sacred and meaningful motivations for working and creating a business, the situation becomes entirely different. It is at this point that, as one economist says, no one can serve society like an entrepreneur. Not even a teacher, a university professor, a preacher, or a writer. Why? Because entrepreneurs allow us to use our time to work, and their work is seen as a "win-win" game for society. But when we look at the lives of great entrepreneurs, what ethics and culture can we observe in them? Let's review some key insights from Kim Woo-chung's book " The Pavement of Every Street is a gold digger " to gain a deeper understanding.

Lesson 1: Work Hard

Immerse yourself in your work, whatever it may be. What is your work? Do you love it? If not, gradually search for work you love. Kim Woo-chung states that during his time building Daewoo, work itself was his pastime. He never took a day off, even when he was working for others. But who can work so relentlessly? It's someone who loves their work. When you love your work, you don't get tired of it. For you, work is leisure; it is relaxation; enjoyment and pleasure are found in work. Kim says, "I have learned not to make work a burden for myself. Therefore, I seek a job that I am deeply passionate about. Once I find such a job, I will never tire of working hard." As the saying goes, the harder you work, the luckier you get. Why not? When you don't respect your work, don't love it, and view it purely as a means to financial gain, it's natural that working hard won't hold any real value for you.

Lesson 2: Don't Look at Everything Through the Lens of Profit

Unfortunately, this problem has deep roots in contemporary Iran as well. You tell someone to work, and they reply, "It's not economically viable for me." Then they sit idle as though unemployment is economically viable. From Kim Woo-chung, we learn that working is an ethical duty; to help yourself, your family, your community, and humanity. It's a responsibility that must be carried out. Look around you; everything around you, was made by someone. We live surrounded by the products of others' work. So why shouldn't we also contribute something to this collective? Sitting behind a desk, expecting high income right from the start, and considering hard work as menial labor that benefits others is disrespectful to work and the culture of work. Unfortunately, the culture of work in our country has become deeply ill, and something must be done about it.

As Imam Ali (peace be upon him) said, "Keep your soul occupied, or your soul will occupy you." Working hard is a way of keeping the soul busy. Those who work hard have little time to be influenced by negative distractions. So work is also an ethical act that helps combat mental obsessions and temptations.

Lesson 3: Limitless Positive Thinking

Kim Woo-chung firmly believed that anyone who is not a positive thinker should not venture into business. A positive thinker takes a 1% chance of success and turns it into full success, while negative thinkers focus on the 99% chance of failure. During his peak years, he was even called a "specialist in turning around companies." Why? Because he would buy bankrupt companies and turn them around within a short time, making them profitable and successful. When asked how he did this, he said, "When others start counting the impossibilities, I start counting the possibilities." This is the essence of positive thinking; a winning mindset.

The Entrepreneur Who Embodies the Culture of Entrepreneurship

When you look at the life of Ali Asghar Hajibaba, you will see that the signs of this entrepreneurial culture were deeply embedded in him. He was extremely hardworking and had no fear of working hard. Moreover, he always looked at the opportunities around him with a positive mindset. For him, everything wasn't just about financial gain. That's why, like Kim Woo-chung, he was able to transform his factories into profitable ventures. His approach to business, work, and entrepreneurship clearly demonstrated the values of sacrifice, hard work, and positive thinking.

Chapter 4:
Resilience and Unyielding Spirit

It's natural to expect success from intelligent people, but often, the opposite happens. Why is this? According to logical reasoning, is intelligence a necessary condition for success, a sufficient condition, or just one of the prerequisites? One of the most interesting studies conducted on the relationship between intelligence and willpower is the book Grit by Dr. Angela Duckworth. Duckworth, during her college years, became interested in this subject and decided to focus her research on it. After 30 years of study, she states in her book that it is not intelligence that determines a person's ultimate success, but rather their determination and mental stamina. The most important message Duckworth delivers in this book is: "Do your children have average or below-average talent? Don't worry. Make sure their willpower is twice as strong. In this way, all problems will be solved."

What Determines Victory?

The message Duckworth provides in her book is that determination is one of the most reliable predictors of future success for our children. In the book, determination is defined as the passion and persistence to accomplish a task. Unfortunately, in the past, it was believed that talent equals success. However, based on Duckworth's scientific and academic research, the message is clear: first, a combination of talent and effort results in skill development. Second, a combination of skill and effort leads to success. Therefore, in the final analysis, the result is: to reach victory, effort matters twice as much as talent.

This is Persistence

Others have written about Duckworth's research on grit and determination, noting that Duckworth is well-known for her studies in this area. She defines grit as the passion to reach long-term goals. In her work, Duckworth has found that grit is a key factor among successful people. Her research indicates that grit is not related to intelligence, but is strongly connected to duty and responsibility. Persistence is studied over the lifetime of individuals. Duckworth focuses primarily on how to develop persistence in adolescents and how to help them in this regard. This approach is part of a broader educational framework that looks beyond cognitive factors.

Although Duckworth herself pioneered a personality test in the classroom, there still isn't a reliable method to measure grit in high-stress environments such as university admissions or job programs. Some argue that focusing on persistence might overlook other important factors like the socio-economic preconditions necessary for its development. Duckworth acknowledges the importance of environmental factors, stating that it's not about which one is more important, but rather that both are significant and intertwined.

Persistence, the Key to Broad Success

Duckworth's research shows that when it comes to large-scale success, persistence is just as essential as intelligence. This is a noteworthy finding because, for a long time, intelligence was considered the key to success. Duckworth says, "Intelligence is probably the best-measured trait in all of human psychology. We can measure intelligence in just a few minutes, but intelligence doesn't show much." There are smart people who don't perform at a high level, and people who, without top test scores, achieve significant success. In one study, Duckworth found that smarter students, compared to their peers who scored lower on intelligence tests, had less perseverance and grit. This finding suggests that, among the participants in the study; all students from the same school; those who weren't as smart as their peers made up for their deficits with greater effort and determination. Their efforts paid off: the hardest-working students; rather than the smartest; had the highest grades.

Duckworth and Assessing Grit in Individuals

Angela Duckworth's work is part of the growing field of psychology that focuses on what are called "non-cognitive skills." The goal is to identify and measure skills and traits other than intelligence that contribute to human growth and success. Duckworth conducted an experiment called the "Grit Scale." In this test, individuals score themselves on 8 to 12 statements. Two examples include: "I have overcome failures to tackle a major challenge," and "Failures don't discourage me." Therefore, you can take the test, and Duckworth has found that an individual's grit score predicts their success in challenging situations.

Duckworth's insights are truly fascinating. Essentially, they can change our mindset about the relative importance of talent and grit. Conor McGregor, the world-renowned martial artist, shares an interesting perspective on this. He says that there is no such thing as talent; everything depends on the time you put in and your persistence. He mentions that all of us are equal, and only obsessive dedication to training and progress leads some people to succeed. Reflect on these words; the idea that talent doesn't exist and that all great achievements are the result of twenty or thirty years of consistent practice and perseverance. While many of us think that talent drives success and leads to great achievements, it appears the reality is the opposite: many champions say that everything comes down to great persistence; and if you have talent, that's even better, but if not, you must multiply your efforts.

Mental Resilience

When we realize that persistence and tenacity are more important than talent, the next important issue is mental resilience. As you know, willpower originates from the human mind. If we have a determined mind, we will have good willpower. If our mind is filled with doubt, we won't get anywhere. One great mountaineer says that doubt and focus are two opposing forces. This means that wherever you doubt yourself or your plans, you lose focus. He points out that when climbing great peaks, there should be no doubt; because if there's doubt, there won't be focus, and if there's no focus, there will be no victory. In reality, all of this falls under the umbrella of mental resilience and a winning mindset.

In entrepreneurship and all areas of life, it is extremely important to maintain an unyielding mindset. The moment we give in mentally, we are likely to give up in reality. But how does mental surrender happen? It happens all too easily. The moment your doubts start, surrender follows and becomes your guest.

Perhaps it's worth reflecting on a novel insight from Arnold Schwarzenegger, the legendary Austrian-American athlete, politician, and actor. He talks about the concept of an alternative plan or "Plan B." You've probably seen that some people have multiple backup plans and think of this as a sign of rationality. But the key point is that, as Arnold says, when you have a backup plan, it means you've already doubted yourself and focused your energy on it. This, he believes, is the beginning of your failure. The legendary athlete points out that you must remain so focused that you leave no room for any other possibility. When alternatives appear, it means doubts about success also emerge, and as a result, you will not put all your energy into success. As the saying goes, success will only come when success is the only remaining option. This is when your mind will be unified and focused, and it will make your actions, words, and external world aligned. With this unyielding mentality, success will come easily.

Unyielding Mindset: One of the Keys to Success

One of the secrets to success in any field is having an unyielding mindset. This mindset allows no room for doubt or uncertainty. Your mind holds various forces, much like the rays of the sun. As long as these forces are not aligned in one direction, point, and path, nothing will happen. In fact, by eliminating doubts, you create a magnifying glass for your brain and mind, which helps unify all these forces. Such focus acts like a lever, enabling you to remove significant obstacles from your path.

This magnifying glass and focus are precisely what an entrepreneur needs. An entrepreneur must remove many problems along the way. Fundamentally, an entrepreneur is supposed to create something new and innovative in the business world, be it a product, process, production method, or service. This newness and innovation require an extremely high level of focus. When a new process or development happens, it challenges older methods. Challenging these old processes requires a higher level of power to overcome resistance. This ability to overcome requires a highly focused and unyielding mindset. As Tony Robbins says, one must have the ability to hear "no" countless times. According to some salespeople, you learn far more from hearing "no" than from hearing "yes." But why is that?

The main point is that hearing "no" causes several beneficial things to happen:

1. Hearing "no" strengthens your progress muscles.

Essentially, hearing "no" acts like heavy weights. When you use heavy weights, you grow. Using light and ordinary weights doesn't lead to any progress in your body or situation. To move forward, you need to go a step beyond your current state. This requires a specific level of pressure, which should neither be too little (resulting in no progress) nor too much (causing physical and psychological harm). Such controlled pressure can guide you from your current state toward your desired future. So, view the "no" responses as these weights.

2. You learn more from hearing "no" than from hearing "yes."

Your career and personal growth progress through learning.

Without learning, there is no progress. The "yes" responses you hear in entrepreneurship and business generally don't provide new insights. You've probably heard that the best source of information comes from dissatisfied customers. Negative situations are the best learning resources. "No"s are a negative situation that you want to correct, and this motivates you to find solutions. This process helps you take steps toward success.

3. When you get used to hearing "no" and don't give up, you become mentally tough, and nothing can break you.

A Japanese proverb says that those who aren't burdened by anything achieve great success. When you can carry the weight of "no" without it affecting you, you'll achieve significant success. Most of us have a weak and fearful reaction to hearing "no." We feel weak, unloved, or like we're failing. However, "no" is a problem of others, not ours. As Jack Canfield says, we can make any request of anyone, and they can either accept or reject it. It's that simple. We shouldn't complicate things.

Mental Resilience is Everything

To summarize, the secret to your success lies in your mental resilience, and everything else follows from it. Mental resilience comes from your determination to reach a goal and never accepting defeat; not even by a fraction. In this regard, train your mind to follow the "no exceptions" rule; that is, giving up is not allowed, not even once. Of course, it's natural to face failure and surrender sometimes, but your mind should not accept it as a permanent belief. If there is failure or surrender, it should be due to external circumstances.

You may not yet be convinced about the power of an unyielding mindset. In this case, a fascinating lesson from the book Hagakure, translated by Seyed Reza Hosseini, might shed some light. In the book, a veteran samurai tells his students that young men should dedicate themselves to courage, above all else. All their time should be devoted to courage so they can cultivate it in their hearts and minds. He explains that a brave man, armed with his sword, will strike down enemies. If his sword breaks, he will continue the fight with the broken sword. If his sword falls, he will use his hands to defeat enemies. If his hands are damaged, he will use his shoulders to fight. If his shoulders are injured, he will bite into the enemies' necks with his teeth. This definition of courage in Hagakure is quite extraordinary; it suggests that a person with such courage doesn't know what surrender means. If he can, he runs; if he can't, he walks, and if he can't walk, he crawls; but he never stops. This mentality is what most athletes should have. As Duckworth points out, losing athletes are those who give up easily. But those with less talent don't give up so easily.

Key Insights from The Compound Effect by Darren Hardy

Now that we've discussed the importance of an unyielding mindset and a mind that doesn't make excuses, let's explore some insights from Darren Hardy's book The Compound Effect, which he discusses in a comprehensive way:

The story is similar to the old saying of "slow and steady wins the race" or the famous tale of the tortoise and the hare. You've

probably heard it before. I believe that on the road to success, I can defeat anyone. The competition doesn't matter; all I need is time. Give me time, and I will defeat anyone in any race. Does that mean I'm the smartest, the best, or the fastest? No, not at all. What I mean is that I will succeed simply because I have two things going for me:
1. I will develop the positive habits required for my success, unlike others.
2. And, I will stick with those habits with consistency and persistence.
I believe that consistency is the most important and greatest key to success. I am a firm believer in this principle, and I have achieved my successes through this.
When I talk to most people, I see that they don't know how to maintain consistency or how to commit to it. I was lucky enough to learn this from my father. He was not someone who was flexible. When I was eight, my parents got divorced, and my father took over our upbringing. At the same time, he was coaching the university's football team. That was when he started applying his discipline to me, and it worked.

Habits Learned from My Father

My father had a very interesting habit. Every day at 6 AM, he would begin his weightlifting routine. Where? In our garage. Our bedroom was quite close to the garage. Every day at 6 AM, we would wake up to the sound of his weights hitting the concrete floor. Imagine how strange that was as a wake-up call. He was always there, at 6 AM, without fail. He also had a note on the wall that he would look at during his workout. The message on that note was clear: "You must endure pain and hardship to achieve success." What fascinated me was that he never missed a single day of his workout. He was not the kind of person who made excuses.

No Excuses Are Accepted

Every day after coming home from school, I knew exactly what tasks I needed to do. No excuses. From cleaning the house to mowing the lawn, to dusting, collecting dry leaves, and washing dishes; everything had its place. He never accepted excuses, unless there was an obvious, clear reason such as severe illness or injury. I am not joking when I say this. Even the players on his university football team knew that unless there was a serious injury, they were not allowed to leave the field. When a player would approach and say they were injured, my father would say, "You play, unless your bone is sticking out." Now, do you understand why I'm not joking?

Valuable Lessons from My Father

The philosophy of my success, which still forms the backbone of my principles, was taught to me by my father. He always said that how smart you are doesn't matter. You need to work hard to make up for any lack of skill, experience, intelligence, or natural talent. He even believed that if you're up against a more talented or capable opponent, the only solution is to work three or four times harder than your competitor. My father taught me to identify my weaknesses and work to improve them, not to accept them as they are. For instance, if I wasn't good at throwing, he would say, "You need to make a few hundred successful throws each day to improve that weakness." Or, if I was struggling with one hand, he would say, "Tie your other hand behind your back and practice with one hand." If I was weak in a subject, he would tell me to seek help from experts or knowledgeable teachers. There was no room for excuses, and I had to work harder and smarter to overcome every shortcoming. And my father didn't just talk the talk; he lived by these principles himself. He started as a coach, then became a good salesperson, and eventually became the president of the company he worked for. He later started his own business and built his personal brand. This is how everyone could trust and believe in the principles he taught.

Why People Lack Consistency and Persistence

Of course, many people do not share my perspective. The reason why they don't; well, let's leave that for now. Maybe they weren't as lucky as I was to have a good mentor. On the other hand, the fascination with instant success and the odd marketing tactics have captivated many people. In fact, we live in an era where results and achievements are expected to come quickly. We live in the age of speed. In some ways, we've become like characters in a movie; we want a happy ending. The issue is not about how this happy ending looks, but about how the idea of hard work, effort, and struggle has been a part of our lives for centuries. Let's dive a bit deeper into this.

Not Understanding the Main Principle

Why are people unaware of the power of the compound effect? A simple reason is that they haven't truly grasped the main idea. In other words, you're seeking a big result. Naturally, you want to take big steps and think you need to do extraordinary things. But the compound effect is a very simple process. You make small, smart choices that, over time, compound into significant results. However, because people lack patience and aren't willing to wait for that time to pass, they give up. For example, someone who practices the piano for six or seven months might be able to play a few basic songs but won't feel that they've achieved much. Or someone who runs for a month might not see any noticeable weight loss or improvement in fitness. People fail to realize, as Jim Rohn says, that success comes from simple daily disciplines. And of course, these simple daily disciplines, as easy as it is to follow them, can be just as easy to quit. It's these simple daily habits and intelligent, consistent actions that lead to big differences. The failure to recognize this is what causes many people to veer off track and continuously fail in life.

When Immediate Results Become More Important

An example I use in this regard is the choice between $3 million in cash or a penny that doubles in value every day for a month.

Most people would choose the $3 million because it's available immediately. However, the penny that doubles in value requires time. The incredible thing about the compound effect is that the true difference shows up in the later days of the month. By the 31st day, the penny would be worth just over $10 million, almost three times the $3 million in cash. But even in the 20th or 21st day, the results would seem disappointing. This is a formula that works exponentially. It's a remarkable concept and one of the wonders of our time. It applies to all areas of life.

Beyond the Possible

It might be useful to look at some quotes from Nirmal Purja's book Beyond Possible. He's a former special forces operative under British command, though he grew up in Nepal. He has scaled many mountains and reached top military ranks as a special forces operative. In parts of his book, he shares some valuable insights:
• "Brother! Just daydreaming about your goals won't get you anywhere."
• "Never underestimate the mountain you wish to climb; I almost lost my life doing this in the Andes."
• "Stop waiting for a challenge or project and get to work."
• "A person's true nature shows during life-and-death situations."
• "They stole my oxygen tanks. I was furious, but I knew that anger could deplete my energy and I would die in the mountains if I let it consume me."

- "Positivity is the only way that can save you above 8,000 meters. No one can fool death with excessive self-pity."
- "I often wondered if I spent all my energy on today's 48 km run, there would be nothing left for tomorrow's training. The training was grueling, and the workload was immense. Instead of worrying about that, I focused on giving my all for today, and I let tomorrow worry about itself. This is the only way to deal with big challenges."
- "Give 100% of your effort right now."
- "When climbing, I gave everything for the ascent and didn't worry about the next climb, because I knew that if I took my eyes off my competitor, there might not be a tomorrow."
- "I did the same with K2 because I knew that if I thought of the next climb, I would lose my focus."
- "Conserving energy was futile. I used everything I had for the climb, because I knew the consequences of not doing so."
- "If I had quit on K2, no one would have known. Many came and failed, and I would've been one of them. But I didn't stop until I gave everything."
- "When you slip, don't lie to yourself. Lies and self-pity will repeat and destroy you. Be honest."
- "I was not born for failure. Even if I'm close to death, giving up isn't in my blood."
- "It doesn't matter what the situation is. Nothing can stop me from achieving my goal, except death or severe injury."
- "Every morning, I tell myself that I will give 100% and endure, and I'll worry about tomorrow, tomorrow."

- "I never saved energy for tomorrow. I knew that if I exerted less than my full effort, I would fail."
- "The toughest training isn't for identifying iron soldiers; it's for identifying soldiers who are flexible and can adapt to any situation."
- "I had a rule for myself: courage above all else. There was no other way in life for me."

A Real Example

This mindset of resilience is something that we observe in all entrepreneurs. If any entrepreneur were to quit after encountering the first obstacle they faced, it would mean that they were on the wrong path from the beginning. If entrepreneurship were an easy field, everyone would enter it. Ali Asghar Hajibaba is one such entrepreneur who cultivated this mindset in himself. Even during the most difficult moments of his life, he never gave up. He firmly believed that as long as we haven't exhausted all possibilities and made all the necessary attempts, we shouldn't assume something is impossible or beyond our reach. Imagine that even when his life was in danger, and when rebellious workers could have led him to a bitter end, he still did not stop trying. If he had given up, he would not have reached the position he later acquired. This is a trained mind that does not know the meaning of surrender. To quote Edison, for him, the surest way is to try again.

Chapter Five:
Patriotic Entrepreneurs

As we've discussed in previous chapters, work has various aspects, one of which is its social aspect. In this context, we are surrounded by products and services provided by others, and our lives are built upon the products and services they offer. If you observe closely, there is no aspect of our lives that progresses without a product or service that someone else has put effort into. Therefore, since we are surrounded by the work of others, we must also contribute something to this shared space. The idea of always being a consumer, without contributing, isn't a productive or admirable approach. In reality, we live in both the roles of receiver and giver, and work can be seen as a reflection of this philosophy. If we adopt laziness and refuse to contribute or provide something for our society, we risk falling into a parasitic lifestyle that depletes both our spirit and body.

The Story of Nationalism in an Entrepreneur

When we examine Ali Asghar Hajibaba's life, we learn that he was a supporter of Dr. Mohammad Mossadegh. Dr. Mossadegh, a nationalist, was responsible for nationalizing Iran's oil and was later removed from power after a coup in 1953. Ali Asghar Hajibaba, because of his admiration for Mossadegh, identified as a nationalist. But what does nationalism have to do with entrepreneurship and striving in business? Perhaps by revisiting and analyzing this trait, we can gain further insight into this relationship.

Here, we are faced with two concepts: patriotism and nationalism. There are clear differences between these two, and we should not ignore them. Naturally, we are born in a certain place, and that location forms part of our identity. A person might be born in Iraq, Pakistan, Russia, Japan, Vietnam, or Iran. The notion that being born in Iran automatically makes someone superior is an example of racial or ethnic superiority, and it borders on fascism. From a philosophical and creationist standpoint, there should be no inherent difference between a person born in a developed country and someone born in a less-developed one. While many might argue differently, believing that DNA, genetics, soil, geography, history, or culture can somehow make them superior to others, we consider these notions to be baseless. However, on the other hand, we do have the concept of patriotism and the love for one's homeland. You are born in a certain place, and that place shapes your growth and identity. This is part of who you are. The place of birth can be weak, average, or strong in terms of environmental, social, political, and cultural conditions, but these factors are beyond our control. We find ourselves here for reasons we did not choose, and it is part of our identity. The first question that often arises in conversations around the world is where you are from.

Therefore, we must recognize that our homeland, the place where we were born, holds certain rights over us. Even if we leave temporarily or permanently, this land is part of us, and it plays a role in shaping who we are. It is only natural, then, that we should contribute something meaningful to our society and our birthplace.

A Gift Called Homeland

In reality, the geography of our place of life is a gift that has been given to us. You might say that you don't like your birthplace, that it's a desert, poor, and so on. However, these things don't matter much. Today, the discussion about the natural and mineral resources of a region is not as important; although if used well, they could be an advantage. Countries like Taiwan and Japan exist today, which, despite not having any significant natural advantages, have become some of the most advanced countries in their own right. In the modern economy, it is the mind, knowledge, management abilities, and creativity of people that are supposed to make a difference, not anything else. So, any place on Earth where we are born is a gift to us; a gift given to us so we can express ourselves. Logic tells us that a wise person does not abandon what they have to look for it elsewhere. For example, if you inherit a piece of land from your ancestors in a village, you won't go searching for land in another area. You have a natural resource you can benefit from. The same applies to the land; when you are given a homeland, you wouldn't go looking for another land to make your own. It doesn't make sense and would be too costly. So, the most natural and logical principle is that you should use the resources of your own land for your growth and the development of others, rather than seeking such resources outside your land. We call this patriotism; meaning you should work to improve and live a good life in the place where you were born. If you think that the place where you were born is inherently superior to other parts of the world, this becomes nationalism and a form of racism.

The Great Driving Force of Entrepreneurs

When we examine the lives of great entrepreneurs, we strongly observe this element of patriotism. Look at the prominent entrepreneurs of East Asia, Europe, and even America, and you will see that a significant part of their driving force behind their massive successes was to free their land from poverty and hardship and to make it prosperous. Naturally, a person can move forward with personal goals for a while, but at some point, these personal goals no longer motivate them. The goal of patriotism and serving the homeland is one of those goals that can provide the right motivation to push people into action. When a national football team wins the World Cup or achieves great success, the excitement it brings to the country is immense; this shows that such motivation can be a powerful driving force. Of course, goals, like anything else, must have balance. If your goals are too small or trivial, they won't inspire you. If they are too grand, abstract, and unrealistic, they will become too far-fetched to be motivating.

When We Become the Reason for Happiness, Not the Goal Itself

You may have heard of cosmopolitan and leftist ideologies. These are things we say cannot inspire others. Imagine you sit in a corner and say you want to serve all of humanity and bring prosperity to everyone; it's clear that this seems neither achievable nor focused. In reality, it seems so unattainable and abstract that we almost have to consider it impossible. However, when you focus on a unit like your homeland, your city, or your community, everything seems more tangible, real, and practical, doesn't it? This is why it is often said that cosmopolitan ideologies, like leftist thoughts, are essentially anti-progress, and countries that engage in such ideologies often don't have a good track record. On the other hand, countries that benefit from a sense of patriotism make greater progress. In fact, we should consider economic development and entrepreneurship as being tied to patriotism. Because, on the one hand, acquiring wealth can be motivating for a while, but after some time, it no longer has the same effect. So, we must turn to higher motivations such as community well-being, societal development, and the prosperity and happiness of others. In simpler terms, happiness is considered a collective matter. If you have the best wealth and personal well-being but live in a poor society, you still won't feel true happiness. This is why it's said that happiness is fundamentally a collective matter, and if we are to understand true happiness, we must move from being self-centered to thinking about others. This "other" could be a community, a city, etc. In this sense, we appear as a channel and path, not as the goal. If our goal is our own personal happiness, it may turn into a negative thing. But if we become the reason and channel for the happiness of others, it becomes a positive thing. This is why many entrepreneurs strive to appear as a reason and channel, not as the goal itself. Some of them have this philosophy from the beginning, while others come to this realization after achieving personal goals and finding little meaning in them. They then define new goals for themselves, and what better path than serving the well-being of fellow countrymen and fellow human beings?

Behavior That Only Comes from a Collective Mind

From this perspective, we can examine the life of Ali Asghar Haji Baba. He is someone who has enough wealth, but he wants to do something for his country. He saw his colleagues who had other factories, and how they emigrated abroad, but he stayed and continued his work despite all the difficulties. But why? Because he was a patriot and had love and passion for his country. This love is what made him resilient. Naturally, someone who thinks differently would quickly gather his family, money, and resources and emigrate. However, this behavior only comes from a mindset focused on profit and loss. But a mindset that is focused on "what should I do" and "what is my duty right now" does not behave this way. Such a mindset is always focused on fulfilling its duty; toward itself, its family, and its society; and once it discovers what that duty is, it pursues it with full determination. This is where we see how two mindsets can create different behaviors. A profit-driven mindset seeks work that provides more profit and ease. A duty-driven mindset looks at what is best for their family, self, and society, and follows through, even if it means facing significant difficulties. In reality, these motivations justify the behaviors that may, at first glance, seem irrational to us.

Chapter 6
From Profit-Driven to Duty-Driven

Ali Asghar Haji-Baba believed: "Only those who consider serving customers and maintaining public benefits as their primary competitive advantage can survive in today's competitive world in the long run. A purely profit-oriented and speculative view of industry is a limited perspective that is not suitable for long-term presence in the industry. Therefore, capital owners and industrialists must aim to maintain a two-way relationship with their community and environment with a long-term vision."

There is a major contradiction in Haji-Baba's words, which, if properly understood, can generate a lot of motivation for you. However, if not understood correctly, it could completely unravel everything. But what is this contradiction? As Brian Tracy says, the primary goal of any business and trade is sales, and the goal of sales is profit; so, the ultimate and primary goal of any business or industry is to make a profit. This is something any sane person understands, and it's not a surprising statement. So, why do we say that a true entrepreneur should be indifferent to making a profit? He has created the business to generate profit, and then we recommend that he shouldn't make a profit. Does this make sense?

About a Significant Contradiction

Here, a seemingly contradictory situation arises, but if we dive deeper into the matter, it won't seem like a contradiction at all. In fact, it will become a great lesson. The real question here is:

How can we achieve greater and ultimate profits by refraining from making a profit? Let's refer to insights from the book Hagakure, translated by Seyed Reza Hosseini. This book talks about the Samurai of Japan and their way of thinking. The Samurai were known for the belief that if you are faced with the choice between life and death, you should choose death without hesitation. But what lesson can we learn from them?

What is the most precious thing for a person? Undoubtedly, it is their life. If you take someone's money, they can continue living. Even if you take their spirit and motivation, they can still go on with life, although it will be incomplete. Even if you take their loved ones from them, they can continue living, though it will be difficult. But there is one thing you cannot take from someone: their life. If you try to take someone's life, no matter how tired they are of living, their instinct for survival will prevent them from easily surrendering to death. However, there are warriors who have gone beyond their lives. The Samurai and their philosophy of fighting and living are the greatest embodiment of this idea. On the other hand, groups responsible for protecting emperors and kings have also exhibited such behavior. Even in our modern history, those who sacrifice themselves to destroy the enemy and cause the destruction of part of the enemy's human or logistical forces fit into this category.

In fact, these groups, because of this mindset, become terrifying individuals, and anyone who confronts them or faces them in battle is deeply fearful. The real competitive advantage of this group is their complete disregard for something that is critically important for others; and perhaps the most important priority in their lives.

An Instructive Story

Once, in old Japan, there lived a man who had a successful life. He owned a beautiful house, had a family he loved, and was highly respected in his community as a prominent merchant. He was seen as a symbol of success. However, fate took a drastic turn. He went bankrupt, came home to find his house burned down, and his family lost. Essentially, every possible misfortune struck him. He became so desperate that he no longer wanted to live. He tried to drown himself in the sea but was rescued. Then, he attempted to hang himself, but once again, he was saved. The people around him wouldn't let him end his life.

One day, he entered a city and saw a crowd gathered in the square. Curious, he asked what was happening and learned that the ruler's soldiers were trying to capture a dangerous criminal. The criminal, however, was armed with a sword, and the soldiers were too afraid to approach him. Despite surrounding the criminal, they didn't dare to move in closer. Seeing an opportunity, the man thought, "If I charge at this criminal with my bare hands, I'll likely be killed, but I'll finally be rid of this miserable life."

What do you think happened next?

He shouted and pushed his way through the crowd, charging at the criminal. Surprisingly, with his bare hands, he managed to capture the criminal without harm. The soldiers arrested the criminal and brought the man before their commander. The commander asked, "How did you succeed where my armed soldiers failed?" The man explained his story, saying that he had already given up on life and therefore, didn't fear the consequences of his actions.

The commander, a former Samurai himself, was deeply moved. He realized that this was the lost wisdom of the ancient warriors; an important lesson forgotten over time. He thanked the man and, as a reward, gave him a large sum of money to help him rebuild his life.

The Lesson from This Story

Life is important to everyone, but when someone gives up their life, others cannot compete with them. In fact, such a person is one head and shoulders above the rest. Now, let's return to the modern world. Why do you think people enter the world of business, commerce, and entrepreneurship? Surely, serving humanity, contributing to the development of the country, and similar goals are important; but the real secret behind people entering these fields is one thing: to profit, to make money, and through these profits, to embark on bigger ventures. Today, we live in a world where, almost, profit speaks the loudest. Of course, ethics matter, but take a moment and think: if you remove profit from human interactions, how many of the things you see happening today would still go on as they are? Now, what happens if you become a "suicidal" entrepreneur and stop chasing profit?

Is it possible?

It's very simple; don't chase profit, position, or advancement. So, what should you be chasing? Have principles for yourself, and follow them fiercely. If you are faced with a choice between profit and your principles, immediately and without hesitation, sacrifice profit. Just like the samurai, who followed the belief that if you were in doubt between life and death, choose death instantly. By doing this, you will gain an incredibly unique and unbeatable advantage:

• While others, for the sake of profit, are willing to compromise their principles, you remain steadfast to your principles.

• While others, out of fear of losing their job and success, are forced to tolerate harsh, false, and bullying words from others, you roar like a lion, and everyone knows not to mess with you because they know that what matters to them does not matter to you.

• While others, because of a lack of courage and cowardice, miss out on many of life's great pleasures and opportunities, you move step by step according to your personal, independent plan.

• While others lack authenticity and live in fear, you become an authentic person, the greatest version of yourself. As a result, others can count on you because they know who you are, while it is difficult to rely on others who, because of fear, constantly change their personalities to chase more profit.

How Is This Possible?

You might say this seems impossible. But the truth is, it is pos-

sible, although it may appear a bit difficult at first. So how does this seem possible?
• You must let go of many of the ridiculous social rules and traditions.
• You need to make the opinions of others irrelevant to you. As Dr. Mustafa Malekian says, do not pay attention to "value judgments" from others, and only focus on "reality judgments." You know very well that most of the opinions others have about us are based on "value judgments," not "reality judgments."
• You must be willing to endure periods of solitude and even being ostracized because you are a "suicidal" entrepreneur, and others don't like that.
If you want to, you can do it. But most people don't want to, so they say it's impossible. Let me explain this in a more relatable way, with an example.
You are a suicidal entrepreneur, and profit doesn't matter to you. But really, does it not matter? Profit is a side issue; the real result and outcome lie in other things. After all, profit isn't the goal. Furthermore, without profit, we can't continue our business, so we must pay attention to it. But...
• For example, you have opened a restaurant and are serving food to people. You need to think about profit, but you're not thinking about profit. Your goal is simply to make sure the restaurant and your workers can survive. You provide high-quality rice and excellent ingredients and serve them to people.
• Other competitors in your field complain. Why? Because they are profit-driven, while you are principle-driven. For you, cus-

tomer satisfaction is the priority.
• Your profit is small, just enough to keep the business running. But your food quality is excellent, and customers keep coming. So, your small profit grows without you even focusing on it. Now, who has truly gained the profit?

When we talk about this way of life and business, we are talking about:
• Duty-centered
• Role-centered
• Responsibility-centered
• Principle-centered

You discover and design your duty and principles, and you act on them, even if there is no immediate profit involved.

And the profit? As we mentioned, the ultimate profit belongs to the "suicidal entrepreneurs" because the best work and highest quality lie with this group.

Let me give you another example:

• You are a TV presenter. Of course, you care about growing in the TV industry.
• The producers want you to act a bit more sycophantic and use the information they provide. But what is your duty and responsibility? A flawless performance with rich information. So, you follow your duty.
• You might not get many jobs for a few years because the producers you've worked with tell others that you're not that good.
• Slowly, you progress in your field and get more gigs.

- Since you are highly responsible and courageous, others know what to expect from you and try to work with you more than with other presenters who fluctuate like waves and constantly chase money.
- As a result, you grow while sticking to your principles.
- In fact, the "suicidal" approach is, without any direct intention, also a long-term investment.

Thus, we arrive at the golden idea that, in essence, forgetting about profit may lead to even greater rewards; just as forgetting to show off our abilities can result in a more genuine display. In fact, business owners and entrepreneurs tend to act with a sense of duty and responsibility. Dr. Stephen Covey, in his book The 7 Habits of Highly Effective People, makes an insightful point about increasing self-esteem. He explains that self-esteem is developed through two things, and in the end, this leads to immense inner worth and value. The first is having goals and achieving them. The second is fulfilling the promises and commitments you make to yourself. In elaborating on the second point, he emphasizes that you create a strong work ethic for yourself, which comes with its own rules and boundaries. These dos and don'ts build self-esteem and a deep sense of inner worth. Entrepreneurs have high self-esteem for this reason, and they do not easily conform to arbitrary rules, systems, or circumstances. Because, if they were to follow this approach from the start, they would simply pursue profit-driven goals, and in that case, it would be more beneficial for them to invest their money elsewhere, rather than in their business. A successful entrepreneur like Ali Asghar Hajibaba understands his role in the industry and the responsibilities he must take on. He diligently pursues and implements his duties. As a result, he not only develops a strong sense of self-esteem but also earns authenticity in his work, which brings him unique advantages. Ultimately, as others are drawn to this authenticity, he gains the final and substantial reward.

Irreplaceability

This could very well be the principle that Seth Godin discusses in his book Linchpin. In this book, he highlights the situation of work in today's world. He points out that all employees are highly replaceable, and this creates a sense of economic and job insecurity for them. This insecurity leads individuals to accept any working conditions within their company or organization. On the other hand, the tasks they perform are often broken down into smaller, more fragmented tasks that others can do for a much lower price, or even for free. All of this contributes to a great deal of stress and anxiety for employees. But what is the solution? Seth Godin suggests that, like artists, we must infuse our work with authenticity so that it becomes truly irreplaceable. This concept we're discussing could be one of the strategies that can help us create uniqueness and a distinctive advantage, making us irreplaceable. In this approach, you bring your mind, spirit, ethics, and personality into your work, and as a result, your work gains an authenticity and a status that makes it difficult to replace. This, in turn, creates significant value for you.

Chapter 7
The Philosophy of Pain and Suffering

We often observe that entrepreneurs and successful individuals in industries, production, and business work extremely hard. It's always surprising to us that those who have so much continue to work so intensely, constantly striving for more in life. Before diving deeper into this, let's look at some tweets by Mohammad Alaei, who shared an insightful thought with his followers on this topic. He wrote:

"I've always wondered why people who have already worked so hard to get where they are have even more of a drive to keep going. Today, I came across a scientific fact about it. It turns out that doing things we're reluctant to do causes a part of the brain to grow, and it's believed that not only the part related to willpower, but also the part responsible for the 'willingness to live,' is involved. For example, when overweight people go on a diet, this part of their brain increases in size. Similarly, athletes tend to have a larger area in their brain related to this than ordinary people. In general, when something becomes a challenge for us and we persist in doing it, this area grows. What's even more fascinating is that if you stop engaging in such activities and try to make life easier and more comfortable, this part of the brain gradually shrinks. It's as though the human body rewards us for facing life's difficulties and challenges, and the reward is a greater desire to live. This truly amazed me, and it feels like I've found a missing piece in my understanding of the world." This idea aligns with the well-known principle shared by Darren Hardy, author of The Compound Effect, who says that if you get used to doing things you enjoy, eventually, you'll end up with things you don't. In fact, doing difficult and challenging tasks strengthens our willpower muscle. Once this muscle is developed and reaches its maximum strength, it enables us to take on even more tasks, because muscles are designed to do just that. This is what others often mistakenly refer to as the "greed and hunger" of successful people. In reality, it's simply their well-trained willpower that drives them effortlessly forward. They need challenges to stay strong and even grow stronger. It's like asking a champion weightlifter why they continue lifting heavy weights when they already have so much strength; their job is to lift heavy weights because that's what their muscles are trained for. It has nothing to do with wanting more or being greedy.

Philosophy of Hardship

Another important point here is that these individuals have essentially discovered the correct path to success – that is, they understand that they must go through hardship and struggle to reach their goals, not the other way around. Let's dive deeper into this concept.

People inherently desire progress, to move forward, and to turn their potential into reality; essentially, they want to become the best version of themselves. This is not a strange thing; it is a

universal need. According to Maslow's hierarchy of needs, humans have the following levels of needs:
• Biological needs: food, clothing, sex drive, and shelter.
• Security needs: freedom from fear, personal safety, and protection from deprivation.
• Social needs: a sense of belonging and love.
• Esteem needs: self-respect and the respect of others.
• Self-actualization and self-motivation: realizing all the hidden potential within.
Therefore, it is natural for people to desire success, development, and self-actualization. However, there is one crucial aspect that causes a contradiction and leaves people unsure of what to do with it. This contradiction is:
In order to realize our full potential and activate all of our latent talents, we need to put in more effort. As success coaches and motivational speakers often say, to achieve things we've never had, we need to do things we've never done before. In other words, we must subject ourselves to a level of pressure that we have never experienced before. Up until now, we've been used to doing things that have become habits. But from now on, we must create new, and perhaps harder, habits. This is the hard part. The question is: how can we push beyond our current limits? How can we go beyond our tiredness and become the person we were not until yesterday? Do we even have the spiritual, psychological, and physical strength to do so?

Running Toward Struggles

Now, let's pick up the discussion here. Until yesterday, we were working with specific, fixed weights. It was natural that the results we got reflected how we trained, how much we trained, and with what weights we worked. However, today, we have decided to push further and achieve greater success. Therefore, it is clear that we can't keep training with the same weights from yesterday. So, what should we do? We need new, heavier exercises, new and more challenging programs, new and more demanding discipline. But, as we know, these will come with pain and hardship.

We often want to avoid pain and hardship. Yet, we must grow because it is one of our inherent needs. In order to grow, we need to reach new limits and keep moving forward. But our current limits are clearly defined; the same limits we had yesterday. Therefore, reaching today's limits will bring us pain. And we, naturally, want to avoid pain. Does this mean goodbye to growth and progress? No, absolutely not. We must grow, so naturally, we must endure pain and hardship. But how do we do this?

Here, it's helpful to refer to some insights from famous bodybuilder Arnold Schwarzenegger, which will be very insightful for us:

• "The last three or four reps in each set are what cause the muscle to grow. It is this period of pain that separates a champion from someone who is not a champion. This is what many people lack; they lack the courage to continue, and they shy away from

enduring the pain, not caring what happens."
• "What we face may seem unbearable, but from all the years of training and competing, I've learned that when I thought I couldn't lift even one more pound, I learned that we are always stronger than we think we are."
• "A beginner does eight reps with a specific movement and with the heaviest weight. As soon as they feel the pain, they think of stopping. But I push past that point, telling myself that when I feel pain, it means the body is growing. When you're over 18, growth is unusual for the body. The body isn't used to doing 10, 11, or 12 reps with the maximum weight. Then, I continue doing 10 to 15 sets in a row. The human body isn't prepared for such a condition, and to withstand it, the body will be forced to grow stronger to endure the pain. My challenge is experiencing this pain in the muscles and continuing it for growth. The last three or four reps are what make your muscles grow. It is this point of pain that separates a champion from a non-champion. I'm not afraid of exhaustion. I'll do squats until I fall and faint. It doesn't kill me. Five minutes later, I get up, and everything is fine. But many athletes fear this, so they don't faint. They won't make progress."
• "The only way to become a champion is to endure these mandatory repetitions and torture and pain. I call this the daily torment because it feels like you have to endure torture. Torturing my body is what helped me look at this pain as a pleasure. Pain makes me grow, and growth is what I want. So, pain is a pleasure for me, and when I'm experiencing pain, it feels like

heaven. It's amazing. People say this is madness, but they are wrong. I love pain for a reason. I never want a needle stuck in my hand, but if this pain is necessary for my champion status, I will love it."

Isn't it great? Perhaps, with Arnold's words, there's no need to continue this chapter, and anything that follows could simply be an interpretation of his statements, shedding light on their various facets. We need development and progress, so we have no choice but to accept pain and suffering. In fact, we must embrace this pain and suffering. But how? Essentially, we need to deceive our minds. What's wrong with that? For years, it has been our minds that deceived us with thoughts of what we can't do, what isn't possible, and what we shouldn't do. Now, we will deceive it with thoughts of what we can do, what we should do, and what is possible. How does this happen? With a fresh perspective on it; by seeing suffering as a sign of growth. If it's anything else, we won't have any psychological or rational justification to accept it. In fact, we must find meaning in our suffering, a meaning that tells us we are moving forward, progressing, reaching the good parts of the story; we are surpassing the limits of our exhaustion. Only then can we give suffering a sacred identity.

The next step in deceiving the mind is playing a logical game with it. Here's how:

• In life, there is no such thing as neutrality; things are either positive or negative, either growing and progressing, or regress-

ing and declining.
- In this regard, nothing we do is neutral; it either moves us forward or pushes us backward.
- By this logic, we are either moving forward in life, or moving backward. There is no neutral or stagnant state.
- Would you prefer to move forward or stay behind? Naturally, any sane person would prefer to move forward.
- To move forward, you must become someone you have never been before; do things you've never done before; have a level of discipline you've never had before. But these are bigger than your previous limits, so you must endure the pain of transforming into a bigger identity.
- Life is like climbing a rock with the goal of reaching its peak. You either climb, or you don't. To climb, you must endure suffering. If you don't climb, you won't suffer, but the reality is that when you don't climb, you won't suffer, and you'll tumble down. In fact, the result of not climbing is falling. Falling is not a choice; it's the result of not climbing.
- So, either way, we must endure suffering; either the suffering of ascension or the suffering of descent. Why not embrace the suffering of ascension?

How far should we endure suffering?

However, we arrive at another contradiction: If we constantly push ourselves and endure suffering, is there a risk of overtraining, exhaustion, or mental and emotional breakdown? This is a valid concern. Due to the intensity of this pressure, you might abandon the desired results and give up, walking away and doing something else. It's important to note what Peter Paul once said: "There's no such thing as overtraining, only improper nutrition and lack of rest."

This is an excellent quote. We are talking about suffering and the importance of changing our perception of it and finding enjoyment in it. As one professional bodybuilder puts it, we should place ourselves under the maximum pressure possible, as long as it doesn't lead to injury. But these things are conditional and require additional factors. In fact, while pushing yourself and enjoying the pain, you must also prioritize the sharpening of the saw, as well as rest and nutrition. Real growth happens after the pressure and suffering you put yourself through, and it happens during the rest period, which should make rest and proper nutrition even more important. Arnold believes bodybuilding is 40% nutrition, 40% rest, and only 20% heavy training. If that 20% of weight training is so hard, then logically, rest and nutrition should be just as important; a fact that most people don't take seriously, and then they talk about overtraining.

Real-life Examples

Well, those were some great and motivational words, but how do they apply to our lives? With a heap of these beautiful phrases and knowledge, I can't even keep myself warm for an hour in the cold of life. Honestly, how does this help me? Now, let's take a more practical and applicable approach. Let's use some examples to come to a better conclusion.

You are a salesperson. Your daily sales total is, for example, 258 units. Now, what those units are and where they are, let's leave that for later. Normally, you sell 258 units a day. However, you want to progress and reach a higher position. To do that, your sales need to be at least 700 units a day so you can get promoted and manage a team of salespeople. The difference between 258 and 700 units is 442 units, and you are currently selling only half of that; 258 units a day. This increase in sales puts pressure on you. You don't want to leave your comfort zone, but you have no choice. You either rise, or you fall. While you're staying still, others are working harder than you, and eventually, they will catch up and surpass you. So, you only have two options: you win, or you lose. It's that simple. If you don't move forward, you will fall behind.

To achieve this, you need to increase your working hours. You used to work eight hours, now you'll work ten hours. Also, you need to change your approach; you used to rely on word of mouth, now you need to make sure thousands of people can see your content in one sitting. Above all, you need to ensure that when you're at home and resting, others can still watch your videos and presentations. You must endure; if your throat is sore from talking too much, you must push through. If you're tired, you need to hold on just a little longer. Moreover, you need to prioritize excellent rest and nutrition. You must provide your body with all the essential nutrients, drink plenty of water, bathe regularly, and make sure you get proper rest. Only then will the pressure and pain you put yourself through be bearable.

Otherwise, you will become exhausted and give up. In fact, by increasing your sales and working hours, you must endure the suffering and pain. On the other hand, you need to, as Dr. Stephen Covey puts it, "sharpen your saw"; otherwise, over time, it will become dull, and you won't be able to use it effectively.

Surpassing the Limits of Fatigue and Pressure

In reality, we must push ourselves to certain limits, but not to the point where it leads to psychological or even physical injury. Until now, all the energy we've lost could be replenished, and it even returns faster and stronger than before. From now on, wherever you are, go beyond the limits of your current fatigue and capabilities. Your limits are where you could have reached with what you have today, but perhaps haven't yet. Keep pushing harder and harder; pay more attention to your nutrition, rest more, and you'll become sharper and more fluid. In everything you do, you face three situations:

1. Current Position: You are in your current condition. This is your present reality, which you can recognize with a realistic perspective.

2. Ideal Position: With the talents and abilities you've had, you have reached a certain point. This is the place you were supposed to reach, your ideal position.

3. Transitional Position: A path opens from your current position to your ideal position. This is your transitional position.

Wherever you are, you are in one of these stages. The philosophy of pain and suffering comes into play in the transitional position, which is created when you move from the highest point of your current position to the lowest point of your ideal position.

Successful Entrepreneurs, like Ali Asghar Hajibaba, push themselves precisely for this reason. They intend to move from their current point to their ideal position, so they must go through a transitional phase. This is why they exert such pressure on themselves. However, they are so calculated that they avoid causing unnecessary pressure, suffering, or pain. In fact, their pain and suffering lead to the creation of new opportunities and successes, placing them in a higher position. If this is the case, then it's definitely worth it. By enduring this pain and suffering, they cause several positive events to happen in their lives:

1. They step out of their comfort zone, and outside this comfort zone is precisely where successes and achievements await them.
2. Their willpower is strengthened and becomes more powerful, allowing them to take on heavier tasks and projects.
3. They overcome their fears. Fears arise when you don't have the power to deal with uncertainties and your current situation. Worry stems from the fear that you don't have the necessary power. Once you have the power, anxiety fades, and you will overcome your fears.

Entrepreneurs like Hajibaba reach higher positions precisely because of this. It is a result of strengthening their willpower, not out of greed or desire for more, God forbid. Although the desire for more success is considered a positive thing in a collective sense and within the framework of non-consumerism, it requires a separate discussion. However, when it comes to the desire for work and success, like that of Hajibaba, it should be discussed from the perspective we mentioned earlier. In fact, the strong desire of such individuals is what leads to greater economic success for societies, and what could be better than that?! As the Real Madrid manager once said about Ronaldo, "His ambition is our ambition, and his growth and records lead to our growth and records." This is how interconnected benefits are created.

Remaining Insights from Ali Asghar Hajibaba on Success and Life

One of my habits is that I never stand still, and somehow, I always find a way. This is one of the great traits of entrepreneurs, and it must be kept in mind. I have this trait in myself, and it has helped me a lot in the path I've taken. So, whenever I encounter a problem, I start thinking and must find a solution. For example, when we were trying to establish one of our companies, we encountered a situation where, for some reason, they wouldn't grant us the permit. We went to a foundry in Tehran-No, and saw that they were manually making radiators. We bought their permit and established the company "Chauffagekar" with that same permit. If we had waited for everything to be perfect, we would never have gotten anywhere.

Basically, waiting has no place in an entrepreneur's vocabulary. You must get your mind working and find a way, no matter what. The key is not to stay still. Just like an ant that is always striving, you must be striving too. If you place an obstacle in front of an ant, it will quickly find a way around it or cross over it. But it doesn't just stop and watch. It is constantly trying, and the amazing thing is, it always finds a solution.

What does a human lack that an ant has? While we are the most honorable of creatures and should be in a better position, the recommendation I have for you is to forget about standing still and, no matter what, find a way. If an entrepreneur cannot find a way, then they are no different from a business owner or a capitalist. However, the main difference of an entrepreneur is their innovation and hard work.

Economic Security Plays a Very Important Rol: It is often said that capital is like a gazelle; with the slightest noise, it quickly runs away. In this sense, there must be security in place so that these capitals and their owners decide to come and stay. If laws are constantly changing, and the security of capital and investment is not ensured, we will get nowhere. It is the duty of governance to ensure the law and the rule of law, and the freedom necessary for protecting individual rights, so that no one dares to change a law and disrupt the investment process in the country.

Sometimes, You Are the Reason and the Key to Creating Something: This is when you should not wait. If you keep waiting for help from others, you will weaken. You must imagine that there are no others and take everything upon yourself. In this case, you will look for solutions, and as the saying goes, when you have no other option and creativity, innovation, and success are your only way forward, you will definitely achieve them.

A Time When We Went to Get Land for Our Company: Once, we went to secure land for our company. They gave us fifty thousand square meters of land in Semnan. But we told them that we wouldn't accept it as it was and that we needed to go to an industrial town in Semnan. We went and saw that, for example, there was only a thousand square meters of land on the main road. Anyway, somehow, we managed to get things done. In one of the country's largest industrial parks, we started the project the same way. We went there and found nothing but barren land; no electricity, no road, nothing; just dirt and empty land. But we didn't back down. We got the electricity, paved the road with others who had arrived, and eventually turned it into one of the best and largest industrial parks in the country. If we had waited for a complete, clean industrial park, we would have gotten nowhere. Sometimes, we must be the change we expect from others.

Dealing with Sanctions: These days, everyone talks about sanctions. It's natural that we can't deny them. We are under sanctions, and we must accept this reality. These sanctions have created many difficulties for us and for industrialists. Here, two groups have responsibilities. The first group is us, the entrepreneurs and industrialists. Constantly sitting and saying, "Because of sanctions, we won't get anywhere," is simply not correct. We must go out and find solutions. This is a reality that exists in our work path, and we must find a way to deal with it. If we are to stop at the first obstacle in the path of industry and production, then frankly, most of the advanced countries in the world wouldn't have reached their current level of progress and wouldn't have been able to achieve anything. Innovation and creativity exist for exactly this reason. We must go ahead and use the available resources to produce and deliver the best products and services. This is our responsibility, and we must think about how to fulfill it. We cannot shirk our duty.

On the other hand, the government and the authorities also have their responsibilities. Thank God, in our Constitution, it's emphasized in Article 44 that the government and official power are not supposed to take over everything. The principle of separation of powers in our country is based on the idea that there should be no concentration of power, and different branches of governance can control and limit each other. Within this separation of powers, there are gaps that we can use to defend our existence and progress. However, the government's main responsibility in this regard is not to create excessive pressure and limitations on the private sector. In some areas, the private sector is really under pressure because the government wants to hand everything over to its own companies. But why? The government has never been a good business owner, and according to modern economic principles, it should be a regulator, not an intervener. The government should facilitate matters, not be the one to carry them out. However, this principle is often not followed, and this has created problems for the private sector and all of us. If we are aiming for development, we must understand what role we, as entrepreneurs and industrialists, have and what role the government has. If we are to do all the work and the government forgets its role, the result will be the emigration of entrepreneurs and industrialists, which has even led to companies relocating; a tragic event.

When Does an Athlete Succeed? An athlete succeeds when they achieve results. What does the right result look like for an athlete? It's breaking a record, surpassing previous limits, or being recognized by credible organizations for their quality in their field. Simply put, it's receiving medals, trophies, or titles. These are universally accepted results that confirm an athlete's success.

In every field, there are similar results that can be used to measure progress. It's about understanding whether the process, path, and actions being taken lead to success and results. The same applies to industry and entrepreneurship. Ultimately, you want to know if your efforts are leading to the results you aim for. Naturally, if you understand this, it will be much better for you. If you're reaching results, you're following the right path, and if you realize there are no results, you'll change your path and actions to achieve success and accomplishments. These are crucial points to consider.

In our business, we've kept this in mind as a measure to assess our successes. It's important to us, for example, to be recognized as an outstanding exporter, as we've been many times, or to receive recognition from various associations and organizations, which has happened to us repeatedly. Does this mean we work just to get those titles? Definitely not; but these titles are somewhat like road signs for our path. You are following a path and occasionally look at the signs to understand if you're heading in the right direction. Naturally, these signs are not your ultimate goal; they are simply guides for you. This is similar to money. Money is not our goal, but it serves as a road sign to let us know whether we are working correctly. We understand that if there is no money, just like without oxygen, there can be no business, industry, production, or trade. Not everyone can barter; money must be part of the equation. However, it is not our goal; it's simply the air that our business needs. The money we earn, the titles we achieve, and the records we break all indicate that we are on the right path. It's like when an engineer wants to build a grand structure. They need measuring tools to know they are doing the work correctly from the start. Without these tools, they may eventually look up and realize the building is leaning, and they'll need to spend extra costs to tear it down and start over.

My advice is to look at titles and records this way: work in such a way that these titles and records are awarded to you. Even have people give you titles, such as "the king of this field" and so on. These are signs that you are doing the work correctly, not your ultimate goal.

It's very important to involve children in your business and factory from a young age. In this way, they will gradually develop an interest and connection to your work and start to link their identity to it. This way, you can continue the business as a family and have confidence that the business you've started won't fall apart anytime soon. It's also beneficial for the children. They will gradually become involved in management and tough work, and their personalities will form in the process.

www.ingramcontent.com/pod-product-compliance
Lightning Source LLC
Chambersburg PA
CBHW071249070526
44583CB00017B/2392